A PRACTICAL GUIDE FOR OWNERS AND BREEDERS
STAFFORDSHIRE BULL TERRIERS

JAMES BEAUFOY

THE CROWOOD PRESS

First published in 2016 by
The Crowood Press Ltd
Ramsbury, Marlborough
Wiltshire SN8 2HR

www.crowood.com

© James Beaufoy 2016

All rights reserved. No part of this publication may be reproduced or transmitted in any form or by any means, electronic or mechanical, including photocopy, recording, or any information storage and retrieval system, without permission in writing from the publishers.

British Library Cataloguing-in-Publication Data
A catalogue record for this book is available from the British Library.

ISBN 978 1 78500 096 6

Acknowledgements
This book would be incomplete without the excellent photographs showing Staffordshire Bull Terriers clearly bonding both as pets and show dogs with their owners and families. To this I owe my sincere gratitude to Debbie Desmond, the first class photographer of Staffords who dedicated herself throughout with great sensitivity and and understanding to what was required for all those windows to the text. My references to the scanning for pregnancy in bitches would be of limited value without the kindly provided contribution of Barbara Wiseman of Wisescan. Her truly expert and pioneering knowledge has provided vital information to any clear understanding of the subject. The photographs of rescue Staffordshire Bull Terriers have been kindly permitted for inclusion in this book by Northern Staffordshire Bull Terrier Rescue. The Kennel Club Ltd of Great Britain has been of great help in granting permission to include much necessary information. For this I am truly thankful. My thanks also to the Heritage Centre for their permission to include historical pictures of early Bull Terriers. Also to all the Staffordshire Bull Terrier Clubs and Societies of Great Britain and Northern Ireland for permission to include their contact details for the benefit of readers.

Dedication
To my wife Barbara Beaufoy, whose never-wavering encouragement and belief always provided such an invaluable source of inspiration from start to finish of this book.

Note
Throughout this book, where both sexes are implied, no gender bias is intended by the use of the pronoun 'he'. This is used rather than the impersonal pronoun 'it'.

Disclaimer
The author and publisher do not accept any responsibility in any manner whatsoever for any error or omission, or any loss, damage, injury, adverse outcome, or liability of any kind incurred as a result of the use of any of the information contained in this book, or reliance upon it. The information contained herein is the author's opinion and is based on his experience. If in doubt about any aspect of veterinary treatment, readers are advised to seek professional advice.

Typeset by Jean Cussons Typesetting, Diss, Norfolk
Printed and bound in Singapore by Craft Print Pte Ltd

CONTENTS

	Preface	6
1	The History of the Breed	7
2	The Breed Standard of the Staffordshire Bull Terrier	18
3	Buying your Staffordshire Bull Terrier Puppy	36
4	The New Puppy	47
5	Owning an Older or Rescue Dog	61
6	Health, Welfare and Nutrition	69
7	Training the Staffordshire Bull Terrier	81
8	Breeding, Pregnancy and Whelping	95
9	Accidents, Ailments and Diseases	117
10	Showing your Staffordshire Bull Terrier	128
11	Judging the Staffordshire Bull Terrier	139
12	The Staffordshire Bull Terrier – Is This the Dog for You?	153
	Staffordshire Bull Terriers Clubs and Societies	158
	Index	159

PREFACE

This book is devoted entirely to the world of the Staffordshire Bull Terrier, and is intended to examine the breed and explore what it is that makes Staffords so unique. From a humble and often violently cruel background, Staffords have long since emerged to become one of the most desirable and sought-after of all breeds around the world. Their superb temperament and proven devotion and loyalty to family, children and the elderly are universally acknowledged attributes that do much for their recognition as a truly credible choice for both family pet and show dog.

My introduction to the Staffordshire Bull Terrier came way back in 1963 when, as a complete newcomer to the breed, I obtained my first two Staffords as pets. Now, over fifty years later, I and my family are surrounded by our many Staffords, some of which are pets and some show dogs. I often reflect on just how little I knew about the breed in those early days. There was so much I had to learn and many pitfalls to overcome before I could speak with any authority in response to the many questions asked by people seeking to increase their knowledge about this most fascinating breed.

My progress through the years has been an all-absorbing non-stop adventure, during which I have always sought to learn all I can about the Staffordshire Bull Terrier. I have judged the breed at Championship Show level many times, including at Crufts, and in numerous countries. Over the years my family has devotedly bred many sound and healthy litters of Stafford puppies, and our stud dogs have sired many Champions of the breed, some of which were famous throughout the world. I am honoured to have spent some thirty years as the Club Secretary of the Staffordshire Bull Terrier Club, the Parent and first Breed Club formed on the very day of Kennel Club recognition of the Stafford as a pedigree dog in 1935.

This book is intended as a guide, and I hope it will provide readers with sound information to assist in establishing a clear understanding of what the Staffordshire Bull Terrier represents: a truly splendid dog!

James Beaufoy

1 THE HISTORY OF THE BREED

Progression – from the beginnings to the dogs of today.

Wyrefare Staffords

DOGS OF THE ANCIENT BRITONS

Attacks upon the advancing Roman legions by savage packs of huge and ferocious dogs, set on them by the ancient battling tribes defending the British Isles, would certainly have made a considerable impression on the Romans. Where had these dogs come from? And who could possibly have predicted their influence on many future breeds of dog in the world today? One such breed of dog, with a fascinating and indeed often immensely cruel history, is the magnificent Staffordshire Bull Terrier.

For many years before the Romans invaded Ancient Britain the boats of the Phoenicians had come to the shores of these islands for the purposes of trade. With them they brought huge dogs of tremendous strength and courage. These dogs were welcomed by the Ancient Britons, who adopted them and trained them to fight. They were descendants of the ancient Molossus, a huge formidable dog from Greece dating back several thousand years and likely to be the ancestor of our modern-day Mastiff breeds. Trained by the ancient Britons and used to attack the Roman armies, they were described in AD 8 by Gratius Faliscus as the 'Pugnaces of Britain' and by the poet Claudius as the 'broad-mouthed dogs of Britain'. Many were shipped back to Rome to be pitted against many different opponents in the gladiatorial arenas, to satisfy the so-called sporting urges of the people of Rome. History records that they were highly successful in their gladiatorial roles. These early Mastiff-type dogs

A fourteenth-century painting depicting dogs set upon a tethered beast.

The History of the Breed

rapidly spread throughout large areas of Europe and were highly influential in the formation of a number of breeds.

After the departure of the Romans from the shores of Britain in the fifth century, the Pugnaces remained for many centuries without marked variation. Among the population they had become well established and domesticated dogs. It is very likely that they were the ancestors of the Bulldog (not the modern Bulldog, but the fighting Bulldog of the Middle Ages). Shortly after the Norman conquest of Britain records indicate the use of the early Mastiffs for bull-, bear- and lion-baiting, which were fast-growing sporting activities.

Around the year 1400 a courageous and fearfully strong dog of extreme courage appears in the records. Developed from the early Mastiffs, they were known as 'Alaunts'. Of great size, strength and courage, these were large, heavy-headed dogs of brachycephalic conformation. They are mentioned in Chaucer's Knight's Tale as accompanying the King of Thrace, and they are almost certainly the large hunting dogs depicted in the Bayeux Tapestry. Renowned for their skills in hunting large game, these dogs were also used as guard dogs and were later developed for bull-baiting. Edward, Second Duke of York (1406–13), described the type in his The Master of Game as 'a short-headed dog – aggressive by nature and able to take hold and often despatch his victim'. From the Alaunt were developed various types of Bulldog, and thus the Alaunt is a vital link in the eventual appearance of the Staffordshire Bull Terrier.

The sports of bull- and bear-baiting commenced as early as the twelfth century and possibly even a little earlier. Certainly from the time of King Henry II (1154–89) baiting was patronized by royalty and had become a popular and well organized spectacle greatly enjoyed by the population. By the end of the thirteenth century market towns all over Britain had their 'bull-rings' to accommodate the spectacles. In the Midlands towns such as Birmingham, Wednesbury, Sedgley, Cosely, Walsall and Bilston all had their bull-rings, as did Hockley-in-the-Hole near Clerkenwell.

DEVELOPMENT OF BLOOD SPORTS

It was during the Elizabethan era in the sixteenth century that bull- and bear-baiting really flourished. Such sports were now the fashionable pursuit of the aristocracy of the day and events were regularly attended by members of the royal family. The dogs they used were huge Mastiff-type creatures, ponderous, fearless and ideally equipped to take on both bull and bear. Always securely tethered, the bulls and bears

Bear baiting.

The History of the Breed

stood little or no chance against the dogs, although occasionally they might inflict dreadful – sometimes fatal – damage with horns, teeth or claws. In the long run, though, the fate of the bulls and bears was inevitable. Their faces torn to shreds, with open wounds, they were taken from one location to another and relentlessly forced to take on fresh opponents at wakes, fairs and contests organized for the benefit of huge cheering audiences.

The crowds who flocked to watch these popular spectacles lived in an age of often bloody and cruel public executions and were certainly hardened to such savagery. However, following the end of Queen Anne's reign (1702–14), these sports began to lose their popularity and had soon almost faded away altogether. The baiting of both bulls and bears finally came to an end with the Humane Act of 1835 which made it illegal.

But this wasn't the end of the story. From the heavy and ponderous dogs of the baiting sports had emerged a fairly rangy Bulldog. Of great substance physically, fearless and aggressive towards other animals, they had already been used for dog fighting, a sport that had started to gain in popularity as baiting declined. Though it was not recognized at the time, it was in this period that significant events were to take place that would have a profound effect on the development of the Staffordshire Bull Terrier as we know the breed today.

As dog fighting increased in popularity, it became clear that the types of Bulldog used for baiting were unsuitable for this new role. Certainly they possessed tremendous courage, strength and tenacity, but they were large and heavily built and lacked athletic agility. Dog fighting required a greater emphasis on speed and agility – in practice, a smaller dog that could move fast and decisively and thus gain an advantage in an evenly matched fight. The upshot was the creation of a dog that was somewhat smaller and more athletic than the existing Bulldog.

BULL AND TERRIER DOGS

The result of the decision to breed more athletic dogs for fighting purposes was the emergence of the so-called 'Bull and Terrier', some-

Bull baiting.

The History of the Breed

Old English White Terriers.

times referred to as the 'Pit Dog'. This is of prime importance in the story of the development of our breed as 150 years later this dog would be recognized by the Kennel Club as the Staffordshire Bull Terrier!

So how did they go about producing these dogs? There is a theory that the original Bulldog was not crossed with a smaller breed of dog, but was simply selectively bred for smaller size and lighter build. Furthermore, the 'layback' in the Bulldog muzzle, which helped the dog to breathe when he was pinning a bull, seems to have been selectively bred out by the undoubtedly skilled breeders of the day.

There is interesting evidence to support this theory. Abraham Cooper's painting of 1816, entitled *Crib and Rosa*, depicts two Bulldogs. 'Rosa' came from the kennels that were breeding what were considered to be the finest Bulldogs at the time. A study of the painting clearly shows that the dog's conformation closely resembles that of the modern Stafford in the body, quarters, loins, legs, feet and tail. The coat colours depicted in contemporary paintings of Bulldogs are also very similar to those of the Stafford of today.

Crib and Rosa.

If this theory is true, then the Staffordshire Bull Terrier is descended from pure Bulldog bloodlines without any Terrier influence. But a second theory suggests that the Stafford is a result of crossbreeding between the original Bulldogs (weighing in at about 60lb or 27kg) and smaller and lighter Terriers (weighing about 20lb or 9kg). This cross produced an ideal fighting dog with all the strength, ferocity, stamina and undoubted courage of the original Bulldog combined with the speed, agility, activity, intelligence and athleticism of the Terrier. The now-extinct Old English Terrier is the dog thought to have been used.

The Old English Terrier of about 1800 was similar in build and conformation to the Manchester Terrier of today, and would certainly have fulfilled the breeding requirements. It is, however, more than likely that crosses were made with various Terriers to produce dogs for fighting. The breeders were not interested in what the dogs looked like and all they wanted was great fighters in the pit, from whatever source. It is more than likely that prominent breeders used their most successful fighting dogs as both sires and dams in their breeding programmes, and fighting ability was the principal feature selected for.

Supporting evidence for this theory comes from regular references in nineteenth-century written accounts referring to 'Bulldog-Terriers' and 'Bull and Terrier'. It seems most likely that Terriers were crossed with original Bulldogs soon after the turn of the nineteenth century.

DOG FIGHTING AS A SPORT

The emergence of the 'Bull and Terrier', 'Bulldog Terrier', or 'Pit Dog', as these dogs were sometimes called, saw a significant change in direction by the sporting gentlemen of the day. Dog fighting for sporting purposes had taken place for at least a century before the introduction of organized fighting with strict rules, which can be traced back to around the turn of the eighteenth century, when baiting began to wane. But this change of emphasis heralded yet another step in the development of what was to become the Staffordshire Bull Terrier.

During the early nineteenth century dog-fighting pits had sprung up all over Britain and organized dog fights, often patronized by the aristocracy, were to be seen everywhere. Strictly controlled by rules, dogs were pitted against dogs, to fight weight to weight. The dogs had to be game and fearless. Huge wagers were made on the outcome of particular fights, and vast sums of money often changed hands. In 1835 both baiting and dog fighting were made illegal, but despite this, dog fighting still carried on. The organizers of the fights paid little heed to the changes in the law, and the practice went underground as they tried to stay one step ahead of police intervention in attempts to curtail their activities.

Each dog fight took place in a pit, across the middle of which was drawn a chalk line known as the 'scratch'. The dogs took turns to cross the scratch line and attack their opponent in the opposite corner of the pit. Some of the fights lasted for considerable periods of time. They ended when a dog could no longer take his turn to cross the chalk line to get at his opponent,

Bull Terriers.

The History of the Breed

Bull and Terrier type.

generally due to severe injuries. He would be declared the loser, having failed to 'come up to scratch'. An owner who wanted to end a fight, perhaps to save his dog for another day, could also 'throw in the towel'. His dog would then be declared the loser.

By the mid-eighteenth century the British public had come to despise dog fighting as a sickening blood sport. The abolition of blood sports by the Act of 1835 had significantly turned people against both dog fighting and those who exploited their animals for gain. Were the organizers and supporters of the dog fights deterred by these changes in both law and general attitude towards their sport? Not at all, it appears, and the following articles of agreement for a dog fight clearly show the professional approach of the organizers and the callous arrangements that applied:

The rules and regulations clearly indicate a cynical disregard for the laws of the time, and demonstrate how the arrangements could always be kept one step ahead of any police intervention. Perhaps, given that so much money was at stake, it is no surprise that 'tasters' were appointed for a few shillings to 'taste' the opposing dog's coat to ensure nothing had been administered in any way towards 'fixing' an adversary. However, of greatest significance is perhaps the emphasis on the gambling aspects of the so-called sport, with no mention whatsoever of the welfare of the Bull and Terrier himself.

Bull and Terriers at home.

The old Bull and Terriers were fierce and dreadful fighters. They were made so by unscrupulous owners, who themselves judged their dogs on their ability to take on and win against any other dog. To such men, owning fighting dogs gave them credibility and the notoriety they revelled in, and granted them a prestigious standing among their peers in the dog fighting world. Some of their dogs became very famous from their achievements in the pit and were very proficient fighters.

ARTICLE OF AGREEMENT:

Articles of Agreement made on the .... day of .... 18 .... agrees to fight his ....dog .... pounds weight against .... dog .... pounds weight, for £ .... a side at .... on the .... day of ....18 .... (who is to be the final Stakeholder), namely the first deposit of £................ a side at the making of the match; second deposit of £................... a side on the .... of .... at the house of ....; third deposit of £ .... on the ....of .... at the house of ....;fourth deposit of £ .... on the .... of .... at the house of ....; fifth deposit of £ .... on the .... of .... .at the house of .... ;which is the last.

The dogs to be weighed at .... o'clock in the .... and fight between ....o'clock in the .... The deposits to be made as in hereinafter mentioned, to be delivered to ....

Rules

1st. To be a fair fight .... yards from scratch.
2nd. Both dogs to be tasted before and after fighting if required.
3rd. Both dogs to be shewn fair to the scratch, and washed at their own corners.
4th. Both seconds to deliver the dogs fair from the corner, and not leave until the dogs commence fighting.
5th. A Referee to be chosen in the pit; one minute time to be allowed between every fair go away; fifty seconds allowed for sponging; and at the expiration of that time the timekeeper shall call make ready, and as soon as the minute is expired the dogs to be delivered, and the dog refusing or stopping on his way to be the loser.
6th. Should either second pick up his dog in a mistake, he shall put it down immediately, by order of the Referee, or the money to be forfeited.
7th. Should anything pernicious be found on either dog, before or after fighting in the pit, the backers of the dog so found to forfeit, and the person holding the battle money, to give it up immediately when called upon to do so.
8th. Referee to be chosen in the pit before fighting, whose decision in all cases shall be final.
9th. Either dog exceeding the stipulated weight on the day of weighing, to forfeit the money deposited.
10th. In any case of a dog declared dead by the Referee, the living dog shall remain at him for ten minutes when he shall be taken to his corner if it be his turn to scratch, or if it be the dead dog's turn the fight shall be at the end by order of the Referee.
11th. In any case of Police interference the Referee to name the next time of fighting, on the same day if possible, and day by day until it be decided, but if no Referee be chosen, the Stakeholder to name the next place and time; but if a Referee has been chosen and then refuses to name the next place and time of fighting, or goes away after being disturbed, then the power of choosing the next time and place be left with the Stakeholder and a fresh Referee to be chosen in the pit, and the power of the former one to be entirely gone.
12th In the case of Police interference and the dogs have commenced fighting they will not be required to weigh anymore; but if they have not commenced fighting they will have to weigh day by day at .... lb. until decided at the time and place named by the Referee, or if he refuses and goes away, then the Stakeholder has to name the time and place.
13th. The seconder of either dog is upon no consideration to call his adversary's dog by name while in the pit, nor use anything whatever in his hands with which to call off his dog.
14th. To toss up the night before fighting for the place of fighting, between the hours of .... and .... o'clock at the house where the last deposit is made.
15th. The above stakes are not to be given up until fairly won or lost by a fight, unless either party break the above agreement.
16th. All deposits to be made between the hours of .... and .... o'clock at night.
17th. Either party not following up or breaking the above agreements to forfeit the money down.

....
WITNESS~ SIGNED WITNESS~ SIGNED

The History of the Breed

With the passing into law of the Protection of Animals Act of 1911, dog fighting as an organized sport was almost completely eliminated as public opinion turned against the sport and its adherents. So how then, did this predominantly fighting dog of the Black Country survive?

FROM FIGHTING DOG TO SHOW DOG AND PET

The fighting dogs had no recognizable pedigrees and the general public had turned against them, but as far as the people of the Black Country were concerned, this was their dog and the Bull and Terriers were readily taken into their homes and treated very much as a part of the family. Reliable fighting dogs could still earn good money and in many cases were treated with considerable care. Their injuries after fights would be attended to and generally they were fully absorbed into family life. Despite their aggressive approach towards other dogs, they were gentle with people, protecting youngsters and looking after the elderly. They were faithful and loyal companions, who never displayed anything but love and affection towards their family and their friends. They never, despite their ferocious appearance and reputation, showed aggression towards people, and their strong and affectionate nature endeared them to all those who admired them for what they truly were.

During this period of general disregard and even hostility towards the dogs, matters were slowly progressing towards the eventual recognition of the breed. A thoroughly dedicated band of breeders, mainly in the Black Country, carefully maintained the bloodlines of the Bull and Terrier that had been built up over many years. Often they faced ridicule for their efforts, in particular from the breeders of pedigree dogs in the growing area of showing dogs. They persisted, however, drawn on by an unwavering belief in the positive qualities of the dog of their choice. We owe a huge debt to these people. For had it not been for their great knowledge of the breed and determined efforts, there would be no Staffordshire Bull Terrier today.

In 1930 the name 'Staffordshire Bull Terrier' appeared in newspaper advertisements for the first time. During the years 1932 and 1933 Joseph

Some early show dogs.

Dunn, the great pioneer of the breed, started to try to gain Kennel Club recognition of the Stafford as a pure breed. He was roundly derided for his efforts but carried on, encouraged and supported by a number of enthusiasts, including the legendary Joe Mallen and the actor Tom Walls. One of the first tentative steps towards breed recognition was the arrangement in early 1935 of a variety show that was held on the bowling green of the Conservative Club in Cradley Heath. Twenty-seven Staffords took part.

Greatly encouraged by the success of that first show, it was decided to form what was to become the Staffordshire Bull Terrier Club. In June 1935 a meeting was held at the Cross Guns Inn of mine host, the charismatic Joe Mallen. It was enthusiastically attended by the most experienced persons in the breed, including those pioneer breeders who had done so much to help gain recognition of the new breed.

Initially, the name applied for was 'the Original Bull Terrier' (to differentiate it from the white English Bull Terrier, a breed already recognized by the Kennel Club, having been selectively bred by James Hinks of Birmingham from about the year 1850 from a variety of breeds, including the Bull and Terrier) but the Kennel Club did not approve the name. Instead, the new pedigree breed became the Staffordshire Bull Terrier: a fitting title for a dog that so definitively epitomized the character and location of the Black Country.

The Kennel Club did, however, give its approval to the breed standard that was agreed on that momentous day in the Cross Guns Inn. This was no easy achievement, considering that all the contributors at the meeting had their own particular ideas of what the new breed should be like. For example, some preferred the taller type that fought downwards onto opponents in the pit, while others preferred a shorter, more powerfully built type for the purpose. Now they had to meld these disparate ideas into a single standard that could be applied to show dogs, pets and companions alike.

They did a surprisingly good job, producing a standard for the breed that has remained largely unchanged to the present day. In the space of a single day, the pit fighting dog of old became a pedigree show dog and pet. It was still, of course, the same dog, but now had to compete with all the other pedigree dogs. Each point of the new standard was agreed and incorporated. The two dogs which were considered to be the ideal dogs on which to base the standard were 'Shaw's Jim' (later to be called 'Jim the Dandy') and 'Peg's Joe' (later 'Fearless Joe').

On the same day the first committee of the Staffordshire Bull Terrier Club was formed, with Mr J.T. Barnard as the first President and Mr H.N. Beilby the first Chairman. Fittingly, Mr Joseph Dunn, who had done so much for the breed, was appointed the first Secretary of the Club, a position he held until 1942.

The first Club show was held on 17 August 1935, again on the bowling green of the Cradley Heath Conservative Club. No fewer than sixty dogs and bitches were entered, and the show was considered an outstanding success. In those early days, hardly surprisingly, the exhibits displayed considerable differences in type. But enthusiasm was running high and the breed was rapidly gaining in popularity everywhere. What a great occasion it must have been for those who participated at a Crufts Championship Show with Staffords for the first time, and saw Joseph Dunn, the appointed judge, award the best of breed to Joe Mallen's Cross Guns Johnson. Indeed, this was a landmark in the show history of the breed.

To proceed further in the standing of the breed, registrations with the Kennel Club had to reach a total of 750. This was achieved towards 1938 and the first Challenge Certificates for Staffordshire Bull Terriers were awarded at the 1938 Birmingham National Championship Show to A. Boxley's dog Vindictive Montyson and to Joseph Dunn's bitch Lady Eve. Further Championship shows involving Staffords were to follow and at the 1939 Bath Championship Show Mr A.W. Fulwood awarded Joe Mallen's Gentleman Jim and Joseph Dunn's Lady Eve their third Challenge Certificates, making them the first ever Champions of the breed. Three further Champions were made up before the outbreak of the Second World War in 1939: W.A. Boylan's Ch. Game Laddie, Miss A. Harrison's Ch. Madcap Mischief and Mrs A. Beare's Ch. Midnight Gift.

The History of the Breed

The war clearly curtailed progress within the breed, but after the war annual pedigree registrations of Staffordshire Bull Terriers increased dramatically, reaching a peak of 13,017 dogs and bitches in 2007 – a far cry from the 147 registrations in 1935 when the breed was officially granted pedigree status. The figures do not include unregistered puppies, numbers of which are unknown. But a note of caution must be sounded here, and the numbers of puppies considered in the light of sustainability, especially in regard to quality.

It is widely known that some unscrupulous breeders, cashing in on the breed's popularity, produce multiple litters purely for monetary gain, with no thought for quality. This often leads to puppies and dogs with problems, and many are abandoned, resulting in a huge strain on the rescue organizations. Fortunately for the breed, there are many responsible breeders who maintain the virtues and temperament of the Stafford by careful breeding along selective and proven lines, producing top-quality puppies to maintain and further the breed.

The show scene for Staffords has changed dramatically. A keen exhibitor can find shows at all levels on most weekends of the year and there are also many such shows on weekdays. Staffords are now so popular that they regularly top the Terrier entries at shows. There are numerous Staffordshire Bull Terrier Clubs and Societies in Great Britain and Northern Ireland and each awards Challenge Certificates at its own Championship shows and also organizes and holds its own Members Limited and Open Shows annually. All this in addition to the inclusion of the breed at most of the General Championship Shows all over Britain.

The history of the breed would be incomplete without a mention of the influence of the Staffordshire Bull Terrier in other parts of the world. After the war quality Staffords were exported or travelled with emigrating families and, just as in Britain, the breed grew in popularity in most countries of Europe, the United States of America, Canada, the Republic of Ireland, South Africa, Australia and New Zealand. In time, the Kennel Clubs of those countries also recognized the Staffordshire Bull Terrier.

What of any changes to the Stafford from the breed's early days to the dog we see today? Changes to the breed standard, most of them merely cosmetic for showing purposes, will be considered in the following chapter. But today's Stafford should largely adhere to the original recommendations of the founder members of the breed, who knew only too well what a Staffordshire Bull Terrier should be. Today's Stafford, however, is generally a more heavily built dog than the original fighting Bull and Terriers. There has also been a change in the temperament of the breed. Much of the aggressiveness of the fighting dog of old has been curtailed by indifferent breeding. A true and well-bred Stafford today will still show what he can do if provoked, and it is extremely doubtful if his fearlessness when faced by other dogs can ever be eliminated. After all, what would he be if this aspect of

Show dog and exhibitor.

The History of the Breed

Proud owners with their show dogs.

his temperament were to be lost? Certainly not the true Stafford of old.

Our thanks must always go to those early pioneers of the breed, who did so much to create today's magnificent Staffordshire Bull Terrier, a faithful and most loyal family dog of outstanding character. Certainly those gentlemen who attended that meeting at the Cross Guns Inn in June 1935 could never have dreamed that the fighting dog they knew would become one of the most popular breeds in the world within a century.

Modern-day exhibitor Melanie Corcoran with her dog IR UK CH Zakstaff What's the Story at Molru – known as Rory.

2 THE BREED STANDARD OF THE STAFFORDSHIRE BULL TERRIER

Kennel Club Champions of the Breed Wyrefare Prince Naseem ('Nas') and Bellarouge Blithe Spirit JW ('Mildred').

INTRODUCTION

A Breed Standard is a set of guidelines outlining the idealized version of a particular dog breed, in terms of conformation, appearance and temperament. They are adopted by the Kennel Club and provide essential information on the desired features and characteristics of a particular breed for show judges, exhibitors and owners. The Breed Standard for the pedigree Staffordshire Bull Terrier depicts the perfect Stafford, and helps to protect the breed from changes and to avoid exaggerated features, perhaps to suit a particular line of breeding, or a desire to placate individual preferences.

All breeders should have a thorough knowledge and understanding of the Breed Standard and it should be their guide in aiming to produce the perfect Stafford. Sadly, the over-popularity of the breed and thoughtless breeding for profit means that there are many so-called Staffords around today that fall far short of the Breed Standard. Prospective owners should read and absorb the guidelines laid out in the Breed Standard, and go to reputable breeders to purchase their puppy. Gaining an 'eye for the dog' requires experience and a competent breeder will be able to help.

All Kennel Club Breed Standards for pedigree dogs require them to be 'fit for function'. This clearly is not appropriate for the Staffordshire Bull Terrier, whose original function was to fight other dogs in the pit. However, it must not be forgotten that the modern Stafford was the fighting Bull and Terrier of old, and other than minor cosmetic alterations and a change in the height clause, to be considered later, the temperament and conformation of the modern dog reflects his fighting past. Where appropriate, when describing the conformation features of the Stafford, references will be made to the 'original function' of the breed, but this in no way indicates any form of acceptance or approval of the so-called sport of dog fighting.

For convenience, the collective masculine terms 'dog' and 'he' will be used throughout for descriptions commonly relating to both dogs and bitches. In the Breed Standard the only specified difference between the sexes is in the weight clause, but this should not be assumed to be the only difference in conformation between the two sexes. As with the male, the female must be of great strength for her size, muscular, active and agile, but built along unmistakably feminine lines. Judges will always rate a strictly feminine bitch ahead of a masculine bitch, all other qualities being equal.

The Breed Standard makes no reference to differences in 'type' in Staffordshire Bull Terriers. Type is defined as 'the sum of all those points that makes a dog look like his own breed and no other'. As in other breeds, there is a range of differing types in Staffordshire Bull Terriers, often conforming along the preferential breeding lines of their respective owners and breeders. Nevertheless, there is only one Standard for the breed and, despite any preference for a particular type, all 'typical' Staffordshire Bull Terriers are judged by that Standard. (It is clear to see that without the Kennel Club Breed Standards there would be little or no consistency within the dog breeds.)

The Staffordshire Bull Terrier is a compact and powerfully constructed dog in a small space. Of middle weight, but not of heavy weight, he should be a dog of great substance in relation to his size. Being neither too Bull nor too Terrier, he has his own unique identity in the canine world.

THE BREED STANDARD FOR THE STAFFORDSHIRE BULL TERRIER

The first Breed Standard was established in 1935, the year the Staffordshire Bull Terrier was recognized and granted pedigree status by the Kennel Club. Changes were incorporated in the revised Kennel Club Standard of 1948, which came into operation in 1949. No further changes were made until the mid-1980s, and the revised Kennel Club Breed Standard of 1987 remains in force today.

In this chapter all variations from the original Breed Standard will be commented on, when appropriate.

The introductory statement by the Kennel Club has been included in the Breed Standards of all pedigree dogs since 1 January 2012. It sets out in clear terms exactly what is essential in all breeds of dogs and cannot be disputed in terms of their health and welfare. The contents of the statement will be taken into consideration whenever applicable in the following discussion of the Standard for the Staffordshire Bull Terrier.

General appearance: smooth-coated, well balanced, of great strength for his size. Muscular, active and agile.

A well balanced bitch, illustrating the General Appearance clause of the Breed Standard.

The coat of a Stafford should be of medium coarse texture, short and close to the skin. In fact, it is one of the shortest coats of all dogs. The coat feels semi harsh to the touch, and is close fitting to provide the dog with an armour-like protection in the face of adversity. The coat of a Stafford in good condition will lie flat and be gleaming. Faults include long, harsh or coarse coats, together with any sign of ruff.

A well balanced Stafford clearly demonstrates that attribute from whatever angle he is viewed, with every feature of his conformation in balance and harmony with all his other features.

Kept in fit condition, a true Stafford exemplifies the requirements for a dog 'of great strength for his size, muscular, active and agile'. He most

The Breed Standard of the Staffordshire Bull Terrier

THE STAFFORDSHIRE BULL TERRIER – BREED STANDARD
© The Kennel Club Ltd, reproduced with their permission. Revised 1 January, 2012)

A Breed Standard is the guideline that describes the ideal characteristics, temperament and appearance of a breed and ensures that the breed is fit for function. Absolute soundness is essential. Breeders and judges should at all times be careful to avoid obvious conditions or exaggerations which could be detrimental in any way to the health, welfare and soundness of this breed. From time to time certain conditions or exaggerations may be considered to have the potential to affect dogs in some breeds adversely, and judges and breeders are requested to refer to the Breed Watch section of the Kennel Club website for details of any such current issues. If a feature or quality is desirable it should only be present in the right measure. However, if a dog possesses a feature, characteristic or colour described as undesirable or highly undesirable, it is strongly recommended that it should not be rewarded in the show ring.

General appearance: Smooth-coated, well balanced, of great strength for his size. Muscular, active and agile.
Characteristics: Traditionally of indomitable courage and tenacity. Highly intelligent and affectionate, especially with children.
Temperament: Bold, fearless and totally reliable.
Head and Skull: Short, deep through with broad skull. Very pronounced cheek muscles, with distinct stop, short foreface, nose black.
Eyes: Dark preferred but may bear some relation to coat colour. Round, of medium size, and set to look straight ahead. Eye rims dark.
Ears: Rose or half pricked, not large or heavy. Full drop or pricked ears highly undesirable.
Mouth: Lips tight and clean, jaws strong, teeth large, with a perfect, regular and complete scissor bite, i.e. upper teeth closely overlapping lower teeth and set square to the jaws.
Neck: Muscular, rather short, clean in outline gradually widening towards shoulders.
Forequarters: Legs straight and well boned, set rather wide apart, showing no weakness at the pasterns, from which point feet turn out a little. Shoulders well laid back with no looseness at the elbow.
Body: Close-coupled, with level topline, wide front, deep brisket, well sprung ribs; muscular and well defined.
Hindquarters: Well muscled, hocks well let down with stifles well bent. Legs parallel when viewed from behind.
Feet: Well padded, strong and of medium size. Nails black in solid-coloured dogs.
Tail: Medium length, low set, tapering to a point and carried rather low. Should not curl much and may be likened to an old-fashioned pump handle.
Gait/Movement: Free, powerful and agile with economy of effort. Legs moving parallel when viewed from front or rear. Discernible drive from hind legs.
Coat: Smooth, short and close.
Colour: Red, fawn, white, black or blue, or any of these colours with white. Any shade of brindle or any shade of brindle with white. Black and tan or liver colour highly undesirable.
Size: Desirable height at withers 36–41cm (14–16in), height being related to weight. Weight: dogs 13–17kg (28–38lb); bitches 11–15.4kg (24–34lb).
Faults: Any departure from the foregoing points should be considered a fault and the seriousness with which the fault should be regarded should be in exact proportion to its degree, and its effect upon the health and welfare of the dog.
Note: Male animals should have two apparently normal testicles fully descended into the scrotum.

certainly should never be fat, and in human terms can be compared to a first-class middleweight boxer. Certainly as a fighting dog, he would not have lasted long had he not complied with these requirements. Today, these attributes are to be admired for the sheer rugged beauty and athleticism of a superb canine, who above everything else displays a confident individuality allied with a desire to please his owners. He is without doubt of great strength for his size. Any Stafford owner who has been hauled along behind their dog on a walk will know this only too well!

Characteristics: traditionally of indomitable courage and tenacity. Highly intelligent and affectionate, especially with children.
Indomitable courage and tenacity were required in abundance for successful fighting dogs, and any dogs that did not display such characteristics would have been discarded. Little has changed from those times and the Stafford of today will courageously display these qualities of his character whenever necessary.

The young Stafford is usually too busy growing up and enjoying life to display an abundance of 'high intelligence', but once past the puppy stage, and fully established in his family environment, he invariably displays high intelligence to whatever stimulus comes his way.

Staffords have a phenomenal affection for and trust of adults and children alike (even in cases where there is no justification for such trust), and it is pleasing that the Breed Standard specifically acknowledges these qualities.

Temperament: bold, fearless and totally reliable.
These are the prime attributes of the Staffordshire Bull Terrier. To quote Joseph Dunn, one of the founder members and first Secretary of the Staffordshire Bull Terrier Club:

> The man in the street asks only for a dog which will not disgrace him by running for a hare if another dog shows fight. But the dog he requires must have other attributes, and in addition mental characteristics which will make him in the true sense, a faithful companion. To my way of thinking, there are three such attributes which the ideal companion must possess. These are intelligence, teach-ability and a willingness to please his owner by obeying him. The 'Stafford' has all of these.

Head and Skull: short, deep through with broad skull. Very pronounced cheek muscles, distinct stop, short foreface, nose black.

A short, deep and broad skull.

Nothing more represents the individuality of the typical Stafford than his head, clearly depicting the unmistakable strength of the breed. The shape of the head enabled a very powerful bite, which was desirable in fighting dogs. The current Breed Standard requirements for the head and skull show no changes from the original standard of 1935.

Not of squarely built structure, the true Stafford possesses a well muscled block of a head that is broad, deep and wedge-shaped. The head tapers from back to front, and accommodates a strong and powerful muzzle and bite. The head shape is defined by the powerful development of a lateral bridge of bone forming the facial area of the skull, by the prominent muscular formation of the cheeks ('cheek bumps') on both sides of the head, and by the channel or cleft that runs from the stop between the eyes to the back of the head.

The head must not be too large or too small or the dog will appear unbalanced. A large head

The Breed Standard of the Staffordshire Bull Terrier

would have put the dog at a disadvantage in the fighting pit as it would have presented an easy target, whereas a small head, especially one that is long, narrow and lacking depth, would not meet the functional requirements of a Stafford as a powerful canine athlete.

The pronounced cheek muscles were of great importance in a dog developed originally for fighting, for which the jaws must be wide, strong and heavily boned in a correspondingly broad and heavily boned skull in order to exert the maximum power in the bite. The jaws of the Stafford are controlled by the muscles of the cheeks. Large and bumpy cheek muscles are very desirable features, greatly emphasizing the expression and individuality of the breed.

Well pronounced cheek muscles and distinct stop.

The stop is the deep and clearly defined break between the top of the skull and the muzzle of the dog, and the depression or indentation between and in front of the eyes. Viewed from the side, the Stafford's face should descend almost vertically from the front of the skull to the topline of the muzzle. The stop must be of correct and sufficient depth to enhance the location, appearance and expression of the eyes. A stop that is too shallow often has a detrimental effect on the appearance of the eyes, making them appear elliptical in shape (instead of the round eyes desirable in the breed). A stop that is vertically angled is also incorrect for the breed.

It is important to understand the shape and construction of the dog's head and the correct proportion of balance required between skull and muzzle. A short muzzle enables a very powerful bite. A muzzle that is too long or too short will not deliver sufficient power in the bite. Tapering slightly towards the nose, and starting both wide and deep, a strong broad short muzzle is essential, with the surface below the eyes well filled in. The broadness and depth of structure is necessary to accommodate the strong and powerful jaws. The sides of the muzzle should display a firm clean outline with tight lips, and no suggestion of fleshiness or an excess of dewlap.

A squarely formed muzzle gives the Stafford a 'cloddy' or over-heavy appearance, while a narrow muzzle gives a 'pixie' or 'fox-like' impression. A muzzle that tilts upwards gives the dog a 'dish-faced' appearance, while a downwards tilted ('down-faced') muzzle is often accompanied by a weakness in the formation of the under-jaw.

Numerous attempts have been made to establish the ideal ratio between the length of the

Short foreface with a black nose.

skull and the length of the muzzle, but variations in type and in head size make this a complicated matter. However, since the early days of the breed there has been widespread acceptance that the correct proportion between the skull and the muzzle is in the ratio of 2:1, measuring from the occiput (the bone at the centre of the back of the head) to the stop, and from the stop to the tip of the nose. This ratio provides an easy to assess and substantially correct head shape for the breed.

A shiny black nose is an indicator of good health in many breeds of dogs, including the Stafford. Wide nostrils enhance the appearance of Staffordshire Bull Terriers and originally would have helped fighting dogs to breathe during bouts.

A black nose is not always evident in newly born or very young puppies. White puppies, or those with white forefaces, are often born with pink noses. In most cases, as the puppy grows, small segments of black begin to form that eventually merge together into a completely black nose as the puppy matures. In those cases where some pink segmentation remains evident, unless excessive, it will be regarded as a minor cosmetic fault.

Not all Stafford noses are black. A dilution in pigmentation infrequently occurs in Staffords that can result in pink, red or even brown noses. In blue Staffords the nose is generally a dull grey colour, with the correct black nose only occasionally evident. All these conditions, although not adversely affecting the dog's health, do affect his appearance and are interpreted as minor faults in a breed that requires the nose to be black.

Eyes. dark preferred but may bear some relationship to coat colour. Round, of medium size, and set to look straight ahead. Eye rims dark.

Regardless of the coat colour of the Stafford, dark eyes enhance the dog's visual appearance and expression. Indeed, the darker the eyes the better. No eyes are fully black, but dark brown eyes are desirable, especially where they are so dark as to appear black. Eye colour is permitted to bear some relationship to coat colour, which mainly applies to light-coloured Staffords whose eyes are a shade darker than their coat colour.

Light-coloured eyes that could do with being a little darker but do not have an adverse effect on expression are considered a minor cosmetic fault. Extremely light or yellow eyes are serious faults.

The shape and placement of the eyes are of far more importance than their colour and any deviation from the requirements for these features is a major fault. The eye of the Stafford should appear as round, a characteristic that is influenced by the bone formation of the face and the presence of a well defined stop, and of medium size. Large or bulbous eyes producing a vacant expression are serious faults.

The setting of the eyes is also of great importance in the appearance and expression of the Stafford. Eyes that are either too close together or too far apart will be unable to look straight ahead. Such differences in setting may be minute, but the eyes are a crucial factor in creating the honest and alert expression that is typical for the breed.

The eye rims are required to be dark, which assists in the dog's expression. However, pink eye rims in a dog with a white coat are not significantly detrimental and should be regarded accordingly.

Ears and eyes that meet the Standard well.

Ears: rose or half pricked, not large or heavy. Full drop or pricked ears highly undesirable.

The ears are most significant as they make a

The Breed Standard of the Staffordshire Bull Terrier

prominent contribution to the overall appearance and expression of the Stafford. Rose ears are most desirable – ears that in a fight could be tucked behind the back of the skull out of the way of an opponent. They should be neat and tidy, folded back to expose part of the inner burr, and depict alertness. They should also be fairly thin in texture, small to medium in size and not thickly formed. Half pricked ears are also acceptable but they must be small and neat in order not to detract from the Stafford's expression. (Half pricked ears rise up from fairly thick cartilage at the base and then bend over towards a downwards-facing tip.)

Full drop and pricked ears are highly undesirable features in a Stafford. Large and heavy ears would have given an advantage to an opponent during a fight. Such ears are a serious fault and are considered highly undesirable in the breed.

If set too low or too close together on the skull, the ears will alter both the dog's type and his appearance. Ears set neither too high nor too low on the skull will best enhance the alert and confident expression of the Stafford.

Lips tight and clean.

Mouth: lips tight and clean. Jaws strong, with a perfect, regular and complete scissor bite. i.e. upper teeth closely overlapping lower teeth and set square to the jaws.

The lips of a Stafford should be tight and clean. Large or over-developed lips are regarded as a fault. In terms of the original function of the breed, such features would have presented easy targets for an opponent to bite and tear.

The jaws must be powerfully and strongly constructed, with twenty top and twenty-two bottom teeth. The requirement for a powerful bite is paramount, and there should be no sign of weakness in the formation of the structure of the jaws. Broadly built at the base, the jaws taper to form a broad front holding very strong front teeth. Seen from the side, the strength and depth of the under-jaw should be clearly discernible. There should be no sign of receding or shallowness of build, both of which are considered bad faults. The teeth should be large, with the front teeth (incisors) positioned upright in the jaws and with the large canines interlocked, with the bottom ones in front of the upper ones. It is not specifically mentioned in the Breed Standard, but the lower canines should be examined for any convergence directly into the line of the gums. This is a condition known as inverted canines. Small teeth, even when perfectly set, must take second place to large teeth.

The correct bite for the breed is the scissor bite. This is where the inside surfaces of the upper front or incisor teeth fit closely over the lower incisor teeth, to just touch the outer surfaces of the lower teeth. When the mouth is closed, the lower canines should be positioned in front of the upper ones. The scissor bite allows for a powerful bite.

The undershot bite occurs when the lower incisors protrude in front of the upper incisors, leaving a gap between the upper and lower canines. This condition can occur either through faulty positioning of the lower incisors (i.e. not upright) or when the lower jaw is set too far forward. The undershot bite is a fault, and a badly undershot bite is a serious fault.

Large white teeth.

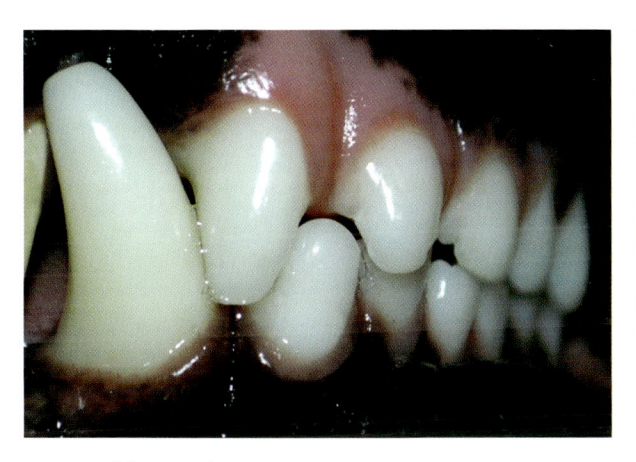

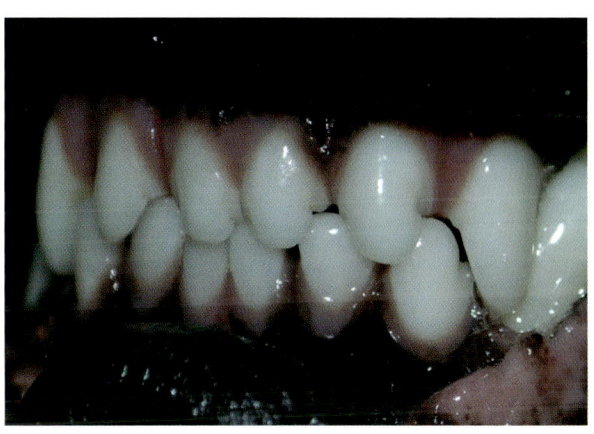

A correct and 'sound' bite.

Undesirable as the undershot bite may be, it is not as serious a fault as the overshot bite, which occurs when the lower incisors fall short of reaching the upper teeth, and the upper jaw protrudes over the lower jaw to leave a gap and incorrect positioning of the canine teeth. This condition is often seen in Staffords with a shallowly constructed under-jaw and is a serious fault.

The level or flush bite occurs when the upper and lower canines meet edge to edge. This condition produces a very weak bite, lacking in cutting edge, and must be considered a fault.

The wry jaw is a very bad fault. It occurs when there is a misalignment between the top and bottom jaws, so that the jaws do not meet in parallel alignment when the mouth is closed. The misalignment normally affects the bottom jaw but can also occur in the top one. This condition results in the upper and lower front teeth crossing obliquely, resulting in a weak bite.

The ideal Stafford should have tight and clean lips with broad and powerful jaws. Strong and large incisors should present a perfect scissor bite. The canines should clear the gums and lock closely into one another, the lower one in front of the upper. The original fighting dogs would strike downwards and sideways at their opponent, an echo of which can be seen in a Stafford at play.

A faulty mouth is not difficult to recognize, but in the show ring it must be assessed accurately in relation to the worth of the whole dog.

Before moving forward from the Breed Standard requirements for the head of the Stafford, it may be worth listing the characteristics that judges look out for in particular when initially appraising the appearance of the head. These include: the length of the muzzle compared with the length of the skull; the relationship between the depth and breadth of the muzzle and the depth and breadth of the skull; the angle between the skull and the muzzle; and the shape, size and placement of both the eyes and the ears.

Neck: muscular, rather short, clean in outline gradually widening towards shoulders.
A well developed, short and muscular neck forms a crucial part of the Staffordshire Bull Terrier's conformation. It should taper and widen appreciatively from the head to the shoulders. The correct neck blends and flows smoothly into the topline of the back, without any abrupt angle or unevenness at the withers. The outline of the neck must be clean and well muscled. A decidedly muscular arch from the back of the head to the entry point at the shoulders is very desirable and will be observed in a fit specimen of the breed.

In Staffords with upright shoulders the neck often lacks a defined muscular arch, resulting in a loss of flexibility. This is often accompanied by

The Breed Standard of the Staffordshire Bull Terrier

A neck that fits the Standard well.

loose skin formation and an excess of dewlap. A neck that is too long will be lacking in strength compared with a correct neck. Necks that are either too short or too long give the dog an unbalanced appearance.

There is a direct link between the neck and the shoulders of all dogs. A pleasing, well formed neck will almost invariably be accompanied by correctly placed shoulders. Conversely, good shoulders will usually lead into a well formed neck. This is an important factor in producing dogs that are well balanced, athletic and agile.

Forequarters: legs straight and well boned, set rather wide apart, showing no weakness at the pasterns, from which point feet turn out a little. Shoulders well laid back with no looseness at the elbow.

Viewed from the side or the front, the forelegs of a Stafford should be as straight as the barrel of a gun and give the impression of great strength. They should be neither too long, giving a rangy appearance, nor too short. Both of these conformations will militate against a well balanced appearance and also have an adverse effect on agility.

They should have well toned muscles and ample bone formation, reflecting the subtle differences between Bulldogs and Terriers. Heavy bone construction is an exaggeration towards the Bull, with additional and undesirable heavy weight. Light bone construction is an exaggeration towards the Terrier and will give the Stafford a frail appearance.

The forelegs should be set rather wide apart. This allows the chest to be both wide and deep,

The Breed Standard of the Staffordshire Bull Terrier

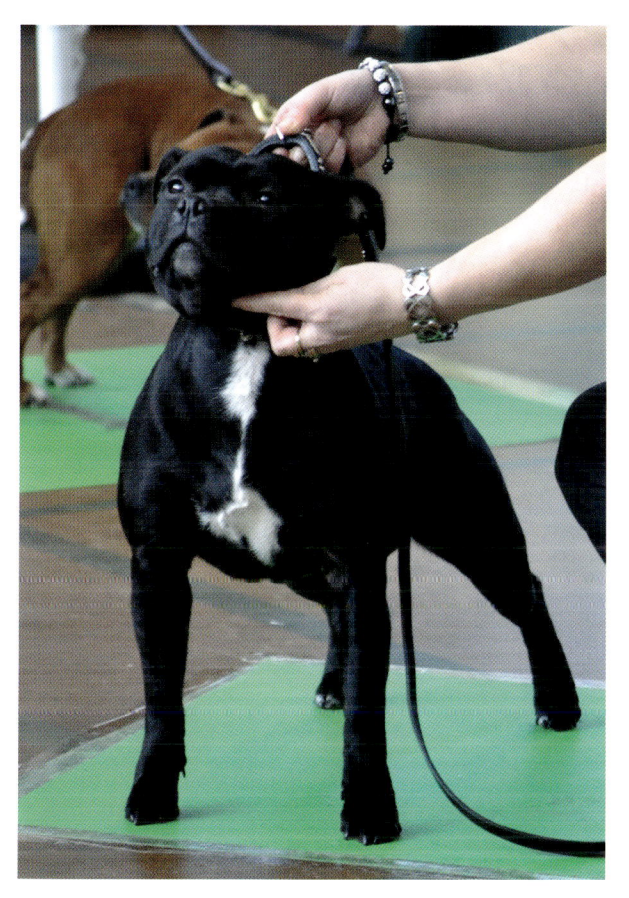

A bitch showing a well balanced front.

with plenty of space for a healthy heart and lungs capable of sustaining long and continual exertion. Forelegs set too wide apart will hinder correct balance and emphasize an undesirable exaggeration towards the Bull and the carrying of undesirable additional weight. Forelegs set too close together, a fault often accompanied by shallow chest formation, is an exaggeration towards the Terrier. Both are prejudicial to balance.

The pasterns are located on the lowest part of the forelegs, just above the feet. In order to absorb impacts they should be upright and springy and show no sign of weakness or sagging, and there must be sufficient flexibility to allow the dog to twist and turn in any direction. The Staffordshire Bull Terrier is one of the few breeds which require the front feet to turn out a little. This requirement emphasizes the dog's ability to quickly adjust his position and rapidly move off in any direction to help prevent him from being bowled over by an opponent in the fighting days of the Bull and Terrier.

Some judges in the show ring, especially in mixed classes with other Terriers, tend to mark this turning out of the feet as a fault but the Stafford is first and foremost a Stafford and not a Terrier! For his front feet to turn out a little is a requirement of the Breed Standard and he should be judged accordingly.

Perhaps more than any other single feature, sound and well placed shoulders lend quality to the Stafford. Without them, he faces a hard task to gain top honours. The shoulder blades are attached to the ribcage and the ribs, held in place by muscles, tendons and ligaments: there are no actual joints. The main bands of muscles involved are located on the dorsal vertebrae and the vertebrae at the base of the neck. They allow for the forelegs to move forwards and backwards, but there is little lateral movement. The triangular-shaped shoulder blades should slope to the rear, fitting closely to the ribcage, and turn inwards at the top to form the withers.

What exactly does 'shoulders well laid back' mean? Much depends on the length of the dorsal vertebrae to which the ribs are attached. With the point of the withers always appearing at the same location in relation to the dorsal vertebrae, then the longer the dorsal vertebrae (and therefore the ribcage), then the more the shoulders will be laid back. The shorter the ribcage, the more upright the shoulders will be. Clearly, if the shoulders are to be well laid back, then the ribcage must extend well to the rear to ensure the desired slope of the shoulders.

The relationship between the well laid back shoulders and the upper arms has a direct effect on the Stafford's forward movement. At the lower end of the shoulder blade, a joint known as the point of the shoulder is formed with the upper end of the upper arm. In order for the Stafford to move well, and with the greatest length of stride, the shoulder blades and upper arms should meet at this joint at an angle of approxi-

The Breed Standard of the Staffordshire Bull Terrier

A bitch with well laid back shoulders.

mately 90 degrees. In a dog with upright shoulders, the angle is more open and thus greater than the ideal; as a result the dog's stride will be shortened and he will lack the momentum of free-flowing economical forward movement.

With the dog standing upright and foursquare, the angle can be measured by placing one hand on the withers (the highest point of the shoulder blade) and the other hand on the point of the shoulder where the upper arm meets it. By running an eye down to the elbow, the angle between shoulder blade and upper arm can thus be obtained.

The correct (laid back) placement of the shoulders not only makes a vital contribution to the dog's movement, it also enhances his visually strong and athletic appearance. When the shoulder blades are too short, then the upper arms are likely also to be too short. In conjunction with a correspondingly shorter rib cage, the shoulder blades, instead of being well laid back, will be upright which will bring the entire shoulder girdle forward and closer to the base of the neck. This is a common conformation fault which impedes the sound gait required. The reduced reach of the forelegs produces a restricted stilted action instead of the desirable economical smoothness. Upright shoulders can also contribute considerably to unsoundness in front by bearing down heavily on the upper arms and elbows. This can result in 'looseness in front' by forcing the elbows outwards, with a consequential bunched up and untidy muscle formation over the shoulder area. This occurs not only on the outside of the shoulder blades, spoiling the dog's flat, smooth, lithe and muscular appearance, but also on the inside of the shoulder blades, with highly undesirable consequences. Such excessive muscular development can lead to the shoulder blades being forced away from the ribcage, leading to a gap between the blades at the top. This produces an untidy coarseness at the withers, instead of the desired smooth and clean appearance, with the neck merging easily into the topline.

Of even greater consequence is the formation of excessive muscles underneath the shoulder blades. This can turn the points of the shoulders towards each other and force out the elbows. This leads to the dog moving with his elbows protruding, or even with his feet turning inwards towards each other.

There should be no doubt as to the contribution to the class and quality of the Staffordshire Bull Terrier of well laid back shoulders and a powerful well constructed neck. These interdependent features, along with the broad chest and powerful forelegs, form the essential conformation of a well balanced Stafford and do so much to contribute to the strong and athletic qualities of the breed.

The Breed Standard of the Staffordshire Bull Terrier

Body: close coupled, with level topline, wide front, deep brisket, well sprung ribs; muscular and well defined.

The coupling consists of the area running from the last rib to the haunches or on-set of the hindquarters. In a close-coupled dog this area is distinctly short, presenting a cobby and well balanced impression. Too short a length of coupling leads to a lack of flexibility. In a bitch with newly born puppies this can be a problem as she needs to be able to turn without restriction to attend to her litter. A coupling that is too long will be weak, lacking strength, and will fail to meet the desired appearance.

A sound, firm and level topline is required in the Staffordshire Bull Terrier. Any weakness in this area is most undesirable. There is no mention of shortness of back in the current Breed Standard, although the original 1935 standard specified that a short back was desirable. Nevertheless the Staffordshire Bull Terrier is a short-backed breed particularly with regard to dogs. In bitches, some allowance must be made for the need to carry and whelp their puppies. In such a compact breed a long back, besides being weak, throws the conformation out of balance.

Along with the required short back, there must be the necessary long ribcage for the desired requirement of well laid back shoulders. A short, well muscled coupling is a prime factor in a well balanced dog.

All dogs have three distinctive bone (vertebrae) formations from the neck to the commencement of the tail. At the base of the neck are the rib-supporting dorsal vertebrae. These are followed by the lumbar vertebrae, which support the loins of the dog. At the end of the lumbar vertebrae is a bone called the croup, to which the bones of the tail are attached. Below the croup is the pelvis. The angle between the croup and the pelvis determines the tail carriage. In Staffords, the Breed Standard calls for a level topline. Thus, viewed from the side, the topline should be as level as possible from the base of the neck to the end of the loins. The croup should then slope downwards just enough from the horizontal to determine the correct set of the tail and achieve that 'old-fashioned pump-handle' appearance. Various faults can affect the topline. A sway back is caused by a 'dip' behind the shoulders. It can

A dog that fits the Standard well, with close coupling and level topline.

A well balanced dog with correct, powerful front and deep brisket.

be caused by poor muscular development, especially in minor cases, but a severe dip is a sure indication of a spinal constructional fault. In a roach back the topline arches upwards, especially over the loins, and the tail is carried too low. Straight upright stifles, particularly when accompanied by hocks that are too long, can result in a 'stern high' topline. Another common defect is the 'sloping croup'. This is where the topline, instead of being level, slopes downwards to the set-on of the tail.

The width of front required to provide for the necessary powerful chest development has been discussed above. It is a crucial factor in the overall balance of the Staffordshire Bull Terrier.

The brisket is the anterior part of the ribcage between the front legs. Given the chest development of the Stafford, the brisket should be both wide and deep. Narrowness and shallowness are not desirable. Viewed from the side, the front of the chest of the Stafford should be clearly discernible, with the lower line of the brisket showing level with or just below the point of the elbow. From here, it sweeps upwards and terminates at the end of the fixed ribs.

The Stafford's ribs should extend well to the rear to allow plenty of space for the heart and lungs. It also allows for the desired slope of well laid back shoulders. The depth and width of the chest in Staffords allow for the development of a good spring of ribs from the dorsal vertebrae. The ribs should be well rounded and deep. 'Barrel' ribs are not desirable. Such ribs are an exaggeration towards the Bulldog and in the Stafford will result in a loss of agility and balance. Likewise, a tendency towards a flatness of ribcage (known as 'flat- or slab-sided') is also not acceptable. This leads to a lack of development behind the shoulders and is a weakness in the breed.

The body of a Staffordshire Bull Terrier, in fit and healthy condition, should always be powerfully muscled.

Hindquarters: well muscled, hocks well let down with stifles well bent. Legs parallel when viewed from behind.
Of prime importance for the Staffordshire Bull Terrier is the ability to drive forward from the hindquarters with power and strength. Back in the days of dog fighting, he would have needed to push into his opponent for sustained periods with strength and flexibility. Each component part of the hindquarters has a vital part to play in ensuring that maximum power is available whenever required.

In order to move forward, all dogs bring their hind leg forward into a folded position. As the foot touches down on a firm surface, the force from this action is directed upwards from the foot, through the pastern and hock joints, then through the stifle, hip and pelvis, up to the croup and the length of the back. As the stride is completed with the leg almost in a straight line, the whole of the generated force is directed forwards, propelling the dog onwards. The Staffordshire Bull Terrier is a very strong and athletic dog, with a powerful forward drive, and any fault that militates against this is considered a serious disadvantage.

Powerfully muscled hindquarters are of prime importance for the Stafford, not only physically but to fulfil the Breed Standard requirement to be 'of great strength for his size'. Viewed in profile, the muscles of the upper thighs should be broadly formed with strong pliable muscle and without any hint of weakness. Viewed from the rear, these muscles should be well padded and strong. The muscles of his second thighs (between the stifles and hocks) should also be of great strength, for they help to produce a strong and powerful driving movement.

Sound and prominent well boned hocks that are correctly angulated and well let-down will achieve the maximum forward reach and backward thrust as the Stafford moves. The hocks are the joints between the upper legs and the pasterns; references to hocks being too short or too long actually refer to the length of the rear pasterns, although the term 'hock' is generally used to refer to the entire structure. Viewed from behind, hock formation should be absolutely vertical.

Hocks that are too straight and lacking in angulation (often accompanied by straight stifles) are not capable of the same reach as well let-down hocks. Hocks that are too long lack correct control of movement and can make the feet turn under; this is a serious fault known as 'sickle hocks'. Over-angulation of the stifles is an exaggerated condition that can cause the hocks to project too far backwards for correct control, and can result in a condition known as 'cow hocks', with a serious loss of ability to drive forward with power.

Hocks well let down and well bent stifles.

Of paramount importance in the conformation of the Staffordshire Bull Terrier is the requirement for the stifles to be 'well bent'. The stifle is the joint linking the upper and lower leg bones and is equivalent to the kneecap in a person. A wider angle between the upper and lower leg is described as a 'straight stifle'. Viewed from the side, it is obvious that the required angulated conformation is missing in a dog with straight stifles.

The Stafford is without doubt a very strong dog, and well angulated and very powerful hindquarters are of huge importance to the breed. In the days of dog fighting, he would have needed all the strength and power he could muster in order to drive forward into an opponent. Well bent stifles, in combination with strong, broad and well toned muscular thighs and flexible hocks, most efficiently provide the optimum power to launch him forward efficiently with sufficient elasticity and speed. Well bent stifles also enable the correct efficient movement required by the breed.

Straight stifles contribute to lack of reach and drive, and engender a propped and stilted action when moving forwards. Viewed in profile, insufficient muscular thigh development can often be observed.

Viewed from behind, the hocks (rear pasterns) should be vertical and remain so when the Stafford is moving. Vertical hock formation is required to maximize forward drive, and any deviation from it is a weakness. In balance with the construction of the hindquarters, and with hocks

Legs parallel when viewed from behind.

The Breed Standard of the Staffordshire Bull Terrier

vertical, the hind legs must be parallel when the Stafford is standing, and remain so when he moves forward.

Feet: well padded, strong and of medium size. Nails black in solid-coloured dogs.
The feet of a Staffordshire Bull Terrier should not be 'tight' like those of a cat, which are short, thickly padded and compact, and nor should they be like those of a hare, which are long, thinly padded and arched in the toes. Instead, the paw formation should be somewhere in the middle: supple and strong, prominently knuckled and with well split up but not splayed or open toes. The feet should be of medium size, with the hind feet smaller than the front. Ponderous large feet present a clumsy unathletic appearance, while small feet lack the required strength. The feet must be capable of instant and prolonged performance.

Black nails undoubtedly enhance the appearance of the Staffordshire Bull Terrier, but deviations should be regarded as a very minor 'cosmetic' fault. White nails usually appear on the toes of white-coated Staffords (and those with white feet).

Tail: medium length, low set, tapering to a point and carried rather low. Should not curl much and may be likened to an old-fashioned pump handle.
The tail should be of medium length and neither too long nor too short. (Check the length by taking the tip of the tail down to the point of the hock joint. If the tip ends at the point of the hock, then the tail is considered to be medium in length.) The tail should not appear heavy or thick. The one cosmetic change allowed in Staffords is trimming the fur on the underside of the tail to assist in establishing the correct tapering whip tail. Trimming can help to disguise an incorrect tail to a certain extent, but it is the bones of the tail that determine just how well tapered the tail will be.

It is highly desirable for the tail to be carried rather low in Staffordshire Bull Terriers. The tail should not be carried high, nor curl over at the tip. Nor should it be curled instead of held straight when standing. The bones of the tail are attached to the rear of the croup, and quite a small difference in the angle at which the croup is set will significantly alter the carriage of the tail. Tail carriage can also be influenced by attitude and temperament, with some Staffords tending to carry their tail high in the vicinity of other dogs. This is particularly so with young puppies, who always seem to be excited.

The 'old-fashioned pump handle' may have been familiar back in 1935 perhaps, but is not often seen in more modern times. Nevertheless, it is not difficult to picture the specified shape of tail required by the Breed Standard. Certainly the Stafford looks good with a tail shaped like a 'pump handle'.

Medium-sized feet, well padded, tight and strong with black nails.

The Breed Standard of the Staffordshire Bull Terrier

Gait/Movement: free, powerful and agile with economy of effort. Legs moving parallel when viewed from front or rear. Discernible drive from hind legs.

Back in 1935 there was no movement clause in the first Kennel Club-approved Breed Standard, although the reasons for the omission have never been firmly established. The revised Breed Standard of 1948/9 also omitted any reference to movement. It wasn't until the present gait/movement clause was included in the current Breed Standard of 1987 that the subject of how the Stafford should move was specified. Movement is a vital part in assessing conformation.

A dog on the move showing the requirements of the Standard.

A soundly constructed Staffordshire Bull Terrier, with well laid back shoulders and well bent stifles, will, if sound and healthy, be expected to move well in a freely powerful and agile gait with little lift from the ground from both back and front feet. A Stafford should always be moved on a loose lead, never on a tight lead with his head strung up, as favoured in some breeds. When moved on a loose lead at a brisk and controlled trot, he should be seen to eagerly respond with a forceful drive from well muscled hindquarters. There are Staffords that move well, but in general, with some notable exceptions, they are not as attractive on the move as some other terriers. Of more importance is soundness of movement, with the legs moving parallel when viewed both from front and rear, with as little deviation as possible.

When it comes to movement, the construction of the Stafford must be taken into consideration. The breadth of his total front assembly, with lesser width in rear, a well developed rib-cage and a lightness in the area of the loins, all lead to the forward location of his centre of gravity. As he drives forward from his powerful hindquarters, the transfer of weight from one front leg to the other produces a characteristic sway in his gait as he compensates for the shift in weight distribution: a movement that has been uncharitably likened to that of a drunken sailor. This is known as the 'Stafford roll' and it is an unmistakable characteristic of the breed. As a result of it, they have a tough time competing against other breeds with a more graceful gait.

Coat: smooth, short and close.

This has already been discussed in the section dealing with the general appearance of the Staffordshire Bull Terrier.

Colour: red, fawn, white, black or blue, or any of these colours with white. Any shade of brindle or any shade of brindle with white. Black and tan or liver colour highly undesirable.

The Staffordshire Bull Terrier is a breed of many colours, and a litter of puppies may sometimes display a range of colours. All the colours listed in the Breed Standard are acceptable, the only exceptions being black and tan and liver.

Size: desirable height at withers 36–41cm (14–16in), height being related to weight. Weight: dogs 13–17kg (28–38lb); bitches 11–15.4kg (24–34lb).

The Breed Standard of the Staffordshire Bull Terrier

Red.

Fawn.

Height should be measured from the top of the shoulder, where the neck joins the withers, down the front leg to the ground. In order to achieve an accurate measurement, the dog must be standing absolutely upright. Although no mention is made in the Breed Standard, it is usually preferable for bitches to be slightly shorter than dogs.

Faults: any departure from the foregoing points should be considered a fault, and the seriousness with which the fault should be regarded should be in exact proportion to its degree, and its effect upon the health and welfare of the dog.

Note: Male animals should have two apparently normal testicles descended into the scrotum.

The message from the fault clause is a clear one. A dog should not be 'fault judged' alone. Rather, a balance of his overall virtues should be taken fully into consideration, with acknowledgement of whatever faults he may be deemed to possess.

White.

The Breed Standard of the Staffordshire Bull Terrier

Black Brindle.

Blue.

Brindle.

Pied.

The original Breed Standard contained fault clauses for certain characteristics, some of them of a disqualifying nature. However, the current Standard clearly rejects such measures. The Stafford should be judged for the qualities he possesses, and not rejected out of hand for his minor faults. It must be remembered that even the greatest Staffordshire Bull Terriers have, without exception, possessed some faults.

3 BUYING YOUR STAFFORDSHIRE BULL TERRIER PUPPY

Owners collecting their new puppy.

Introducing a Staffordshire Bull Terrier puppy into your life and family home is an emotional and rewarding experience, but it is an undertaking that must be approached with common sense, caution and planning. Before you commit to taking on a puppy, you should spend time researching the breed and making sure you can provide a good home for the new arrival. One of the most important considerations is whether a Stafford puppy would suit your home and lifestyle. A puppy needs kindness, human companionship, a place to sleep, regular meals and exercise. He will adapt to just about any form of accommo-dation.

You should also take into account some other aspects of owning a puppy, not least the level of security provided by your premises. Whether you live in a house with a garden, a flat, a maisonette, or even a country estate, it is important to ensure your puppy's welfare. Puppies are naturally inquisitive and like nothing more than wriggling through a hole in a fence to find out what's on the other side. Nor can they resist the challenge of an unknown cat or dog intruding into his territory.

The presence of other family pets in the home is an important factor. Staffords generally do not like other dogs outside the home environment, especially so if those dogs show any aggression towards them, but within the home a Stafford usually makes a good friend and companion for

At eight weeks it's all so new.

another dog, particularly if of the opposite sex. Also of course, provided no jealousy is allowed to arise, perhaps through favouritism or issues over food. Dogs and cats are natural enemies, and woe betide any cat intruding into your Stafford's territory. But it's usually a different matter when it comes to the family cat. After a 'settling down period', your cat and your Stafford will often become the firmest of friends.

Another consideration is how the puppy would fit physically into your own environment. One essential requirement is for an easily accessible area for the puppy's toilet requirements. He will also need a separate place with suitable bedding for uninterrupted sleeping, and of course somewhere for feeding at mealtimes.

Dog and bitch puppies at seven weeks old.

Would a Staffordshire Bull Terrier fit into your lifestyle? There is more to keeping a dog healthy and happy than providing for his well-being in the home. What about exercise? As your puppy grows, he will need daily attention to keep healthy and fit, and when he is older he will need regular walks. When you and your family go away on holidays, or for long weekends, will you take your Stafford with you or arrange for him to be looked after in your absence? Have you considered the costs of feeding, vaccinations and veterinary care? All these questions should be addressed before making the commitment to buy a puppy. Only then can you proceed with confidence to select your new friend.

Before buying a puppy, you must decide whether you want a show-quality Stafford for exhibiting at dog shows or if you simply want a pet and companion. Tell the breeder of your prospective puppy at the outset, as this will help them help you make the right choice. From a well bred litter, it is reasonable to assume the purchase price will be reduced for a puppy that may have a slight fault which precludes that puppy from exhibiting at a dog show. A responsible breeder will be able to advise you on each puppy's temperament and qualities.

DOG OR BITCH?

All Staffords, whether dogs or bitches, make very rewarding additions to your home. Strong and powerful, they will protect the whole family, in particular the young and the elderly. They are entirely devoted to their owners, and well bred dogs will demonstrate the reliability and soundness of temperament expected of the breed.

If a dog is selected as a show prospect, particularly if he turns out to be a good one, then you are in for exciting times! A well bred dog that is successful in the show ring will be much in demand among breeders who wish to use him for stud services with their bitches. But if he does not mature into a successful show dog, you must accept him as the family dog and pet for the rest of his life. For someone who simply wants a pet and companion, lack of success in the show ring is not a problem, as the dog will be exactly what was wanted in the first place. Whether show prospect or pet, the Stafford is a dog that you can be proud of.

It is entirely a matter of personal preference, of course, but a bitch puppy may be a wiser choice, especially for an inexperienced owner. Bitches

Buying your Staffordshire Bull Terrier Puppy

in general can be more easily handled than a stronger and more boisterous dog, and often prove more biddable in the home environment. Tremendously faithful to her family, she will naturally guard all members of the household, demonstrating a loyalty that cannot be surpassed. A good show bitch will often excel in the show ring, even against the top male exhibits, and puppies from a successful bitch will be greatly in demand. For those who wish to compete in the show ring, one of the biggest advantages of choosing a bitch is that even if she does not excel as a show dog, she can be mated to a top stud dog to produce a potential show prospect that her owner could then campaign.

Bitches naturally come into season twice yearly for three weeks each time, and during these periods it is important to ensure that they are not able to mate accidentally. But this is a small inconvenience, compared with the advantages of owning a beautiful and loyal Stafford bitch.

The choice of dog or bitch is very much a matter of personal preference. A male dog, though often stronger and more assertive than a female, will not necessarily be dominant. A bitch, when roused or threatened, is more than capable of holding her own: a match, in fact, for any dog! Whether you want a show dog or a pet, doing your research and going about it in the right way will increase your chances of becoming the owner of a magnificent canine that you will always be proud of, and that will always give you far more love than you will ever be able to return.

Should you be looking for a guard dog, don't consider a Stafford as you will be disappointed. The Stafford, though strong and fearless, would not be the dog for you. Any aggression in a true Stafford will be directed only towards other dogs and not towards persons. Should a burglar gain access to your premises, your Stafford, rather than going on the attack, would be more likely to lead him to your refrigerator. Such is the Stafford's trust in people! If you want a guard dog, your best bet is to consider breeds trained for the purpose.

However, a true Stafford dog or bitch will not stand any nonsense from other dogs that try to bully them. Staffords in these circumstances are more than capable of showing what a big mistake the aggressor has made. This, of course, can get you into trouble with an irate owner who rarely blames his own dog, even when that dog is running loose and charges in on your Stafford. Always the Stafford is seen to be at fault, even if he is securely controlled on a lead. The message is clear: always keep your Stafford on a lead in public places where other dogs may be running around freely. It is not worth running even the slightest risk of any form of aggression between your Stafford and other dogs, resulting in injury or potentially fatal consequences. Any infringement of the provisions of the Dangerous Dogs Act may lead to tragedy and grief.

Dog and bitch puppies at play (five weeks old).

KENNEL CLUB REGISTRATION

Whether show prospect or pet, and whether dog or bitch, it is strongly advised that you buy a Kennel Club registered pedigree Staffordshire Bull Terrier puppy. The consequences of purchasing unregistered puppies, or those registered by unofficial sources, could be dire. A puppy without official Kennel Club registration can never be entered for an officially recognized dog show. Furthermore, any puppies born from an unregistered sire or dam can never be registered as pedigree Staffordshire Bull Terriers, and would never be acknowledged to be of pedigree status. There is only one true pedigree Staffordshire Bull Terrier and that is a Kennel Club registered Staffordshire Bull Terrier.

Why purchase a Stafford that is not Kennel Club registered when it is not difficult to obtain one that is? Do not fall into the trap of the 'uncaring exploiting the uninformed'. Instead, take the trouble to learn all you can about the breed and then approach reputable breeders of true pedigree Staffordshire Bull Terriers.

FINDING A PUPPY

Having made up your mind that a Staffordshire Bull Terrier puppy is for you, the next step is to decide how you are going to go about it in order to accomplish exactly what you are looking for. Hopefully by this stage you will already have learned much about the breed. Always go to a reputable breeder, and avoid buying a puppy in haste or on impulse or for the wrong reasons.

There are officially recognized Staffordshire Bull Terrier Clubs in all areas of the country. Details can be obtained through the Kennel Club. The Secretary of your local club will be able to advise you on many areas, and point you in the direction of local dog shows. One of the best ways to learn about Staffords is to go along to as many

Healthy, happy puppies at play.

Buying your Staffordshire Bull Terrier Puppy

dog shows as possible, to see for yourself the very best Stafford dogs and bitches and to talk with experienced owners. Such people may well be able to advise you of any pedigree Stafford litters available or expected. Often expected well bred litters are advertised in show catalogues, enabling you to make contact with the breeder at that show and look at their other dogs. Tempting though it may be, don't make up your mind too soon; try to see as many dogs and bitches as possible to help you form your own opinion of exactly what it is you're looking for. The Secretary of your local club will also be able to tell you about any Stafford training clubs in the area. You can go along to these and get a good, close look at the Staffords there. This can be a very good way to obtain a puppy for yourself, as at shows or training classes you may well find an experienced person who will help you.

Seek the advice of as many different Staffordshire Bull Terrier owners, judges and breeders as you can before you make up your mind. They will be at the shows and training clubs. The top breeders rarely advertise their puppies. These people breed with the purpose of furthering and improving their own stock, and will be looking for homes for the well bred puppies they will not be keeping for themselves. Obtaining your puppy from them is probably the best way to fulfil your requirements. You can contact them through your Staffordshire Bull Terrier Club, and at shows.

Another excellent way to obtain a Stafford puppy is through the Kennel Club's Assured Breeders Scheme.

Potential owners should exercise extreme caution before responding to Stafford advertisements in local papers. Would you be making contact with a genuine Staffordshire Bull Terrier breeder? Or a person who has simply bred a litter to make money for themselves. Unfortunately such unscrupulous people have little regard for the welfare of the puppies once they have been sold. Would the puppies advertised as Staffords be the genuine article, or cross-bred non-registered dogs and bitches with Stafford blood somewhere in their backgrounds? Would you expect to get as good after-sales assistance as you would from a genuine breeder? Would you be getting a genuine Kennel Club registered pedigree puppy for your money?

Likewise, **never** buy a Staffordshire Bull Terrier (or what passes as a Staffordshire Bull Terrier) from a pet shop or puppy farm. The likelihood is that such puppies will be poorly bred and possibly unhealthy. They will almost certainly not have been weaned and socialized properly, and it is extremely doubtful that they will be Kennel Club registered as pedigree animals, regardless of any paperwork you may be offered.

Stay well away from any puppies described as 'Pompy Staffords', 'Irish Staffords', 'King Staffords' or 'Original Staffords' – in fact, avoid anything that is not a true Staffordshire Bull Terrier. Such dogs are generally cross-bred, with some Stafford blood in their background. They are not genuine Staffordshire Bull Terriers. Resist the temptation to purchase a Stafford that is advertised as being 'rare' and thus is being sold at an inflated price because it is 'special'. There is no such thing as a 'rare' Staffordshire Bull Terrier.

A good example of a well bred Stafford puppy.

Reproduced by kind permission of the Kennel Club

THE KENNEL CLUB ASSURED BREEDERS SCHEME

The aim of the Kennel Club Assured Breeders Scheme is to promote responsible breeding practices. There are twelve specific requirements that Kennel Club Assured Breeders must fulfil:

1. Ensure that all breeding stock is Kennel Club registered, and take all reasonable steps to ensure that the dogs are healthy and able to function normally (i.e. fit for function for life).

2. Hand over the puppy's registration certificate at the time of sale, if available, or forward it to the new owner as soon as possible. Explain any endorsements that might pertain, and obtain written and signed confirmation from the new owner, at or before the date on which ownership is transferred, that the new owner is aware of the endorsement(s), regardless of whether or not the endorsed registration certificate is available.

3. Follow Kennel Club policy regarding the maximum number and frequency of litters.

4. Permanently identify breeding stock owned or offered at stud by DNA profile, microchip or tattoo. (NB: at some stage all breeding stock will need to be DNA profiled.)

5. Make use of Kennel Club health screening schemes, relevant to their breed, on all breeding stock owned or offered at stud. These schemes include DNA testing, hip dysplasia, elbow dysplasia and inherited eye conditions. No mating must take place if the relevant test results indicate that it would be inadvisable in the sense that it is likely to produce health or welfare problems in the offspring and/or it is inadvisable in the context of a relevant breeding strategy. The current list of checks can be found at www.thekennelclub.org.uk/download/1100/abshealthregs.pdf.

6. Give written, breed-specific advice to puppy buyers in a Puppy Sales Wallet concerning (a) tendencies and potential traits in the breed; (b) socialisation, exercise and training; (c) feeding and worming programmes; and (d) grooming.

7. Inform the new owner in writing of any vaccinations that have been carried out.

8. Provide reasonable post-sales telephone advice and endeavour to deal in good faith with any issues that may arise.

9. Inform the new owner about the requirements and recommendations that apply to Kennel Club Assured Breeders, as well as drawing attention to the existence of the complaints procedure.

10. Draw up a contract of sale for each puppy sold and provide a copy in the Puppy Sales Wallet.

11. All dogs offered for breeding must be subject to the rules of the Assured Breeder Scheme.

12. Draw up a Contract of Stud Dog Service for each service performed and include details and results of all relevant health tests performed in accordance with the Assured Breeders Scheme.

For more information check the website, email abs@thekennelclub.org.uk, or call the Assured Breeders Scheme department directly on 020 7518 1015.

VISITING THE BREEDER

When you visit your selected breeder to see the litter of puppies, take the opportunity to ask any questions you may have. Try to go with your family and any other persons who will be involved with looking after the new puppy. Unless you are experienced enough yourself, it would be helpful to take along someone who is well qualified to assess Staffordshire Bull Terrier puppies and advise you accordingly. Remember, it won't be just you asking questions. Responsible breeders will want to be satisfied that you are the right person to have one of their puppies.

Puppies should not go to their new homes before they are at least eight weeks old. They must be allowed to spend sufficient time with their mother and to have had plenty of experience with human beings. The bitch will not only have fed and taken care of her puppies, but also have taught them what puppies need to know about acceptable behaviour and the language of dogs. A puppy taken away from his mother too early will not have learned to understand other dogs, and this may result in problems with socialization as he grows up.

Stafford puppies start the socializing process at about three weeks old, and the next two to three weeks are the critical period. During this time they will become fully aware of their mother and their litter mates, human beings and any other dogs or pets in the home. They will be attracted to just about anything they come across and will learn from it all and retain that information. They utilize all their senses, particularly that of smell, to adapt it to their environment. It is important to ensure that your puppy has been reared in an atmosphere of activity and noise, with plenty of human exposure, as he will benefit from such an upbringing for the rest of his life. A puppy that has spent his formative weeks in quiet surroundings with not much to stimulate his senses and insufficient human contact will lack confidence and the necessary skills to achieve a well balanced and active life.

A sensible breeder will not allow prospective new owners to view a litter of puppies at too early an age. This can cause the bitch distress, with possibly tragic consequences should she instinctively react to protect her young. From the age of four weeks onwards the puppies will be much more aware of their surroundings and

Puppies ready for their new families.

Buying your Staffordshire Bull Terrier Puppy

A new owner beginning to bond with her puppy at four weeks.

will be running around busily. At this stage the bitch will be much more open to the attentions of strangers.

The purchase of a puppy at eight weeks of age is always something of a gamble, as no one can be sure how an individual puppy will mature. The odds of obtaining a sound and healthy dog can, however, be substantially reduced in favour of the purchaser by following the advice given above. Responsible breeders will also help you with your selection, without taking advantage of your inexperience. Do, however, beware of any false claims that may be introduced into the proceedings.

Before going to look at a litter of puppies, it is sensible to discuss and agree the financial arrangements for a potential purchase. A deposit is often required, and it needs to be ascertained whether this is returnable if a sale does not materialize.

During your first visit, take the opportunity to observe the circumstances and conditions in which the puppies have been raised. You need to be satisfied that all is well and the puppies

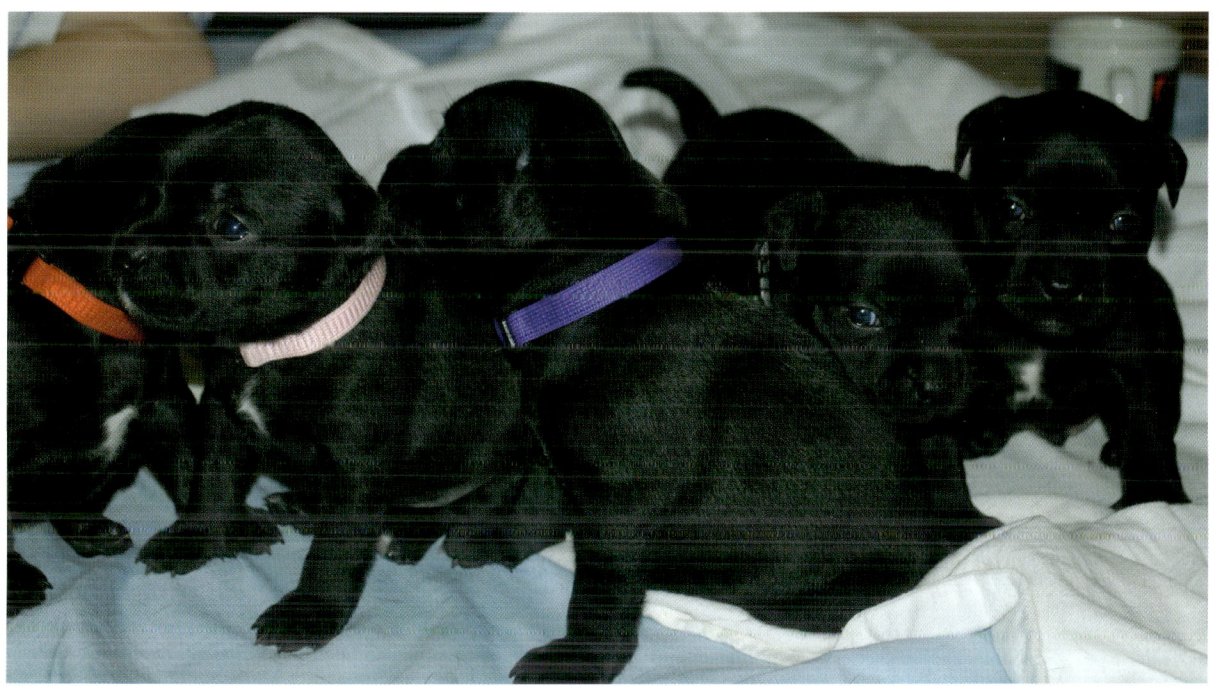

The puppies should be confident and ready for their first visitors at around four or five weeks.

Buying your Staffordshire Bull Terrier Puppy

A litter content with their dam.

are thriving in their environment. If you have any doubts, then either proceed with caution or approach another breeder. Always ask to see the pedigree of the puppies, and find out if they are, or will be, registered with the Kennel Club. There should be no problems with these matters if you have approached a responsible breeder.

Whether you are looking for a pet or a dog with show prospects, the intention should be exactly the same: to obtain a clearly healthy and 'typical' Staffordshire Bull Terrier puppy. Always ask to see all the puppies in a litter as this will give the best chance to see them running about and playing together. It also allows comparisons to be made. (Do not be deterred if there is only a single puppy, providing it is strong and healthy. Single puppies can often become stars of the showing world when they mature.) Ask to see the bitch, and, if possible, the sire also.

The mother may naturally be showing some signs of debilitation brought about by the raising and feeding of her litter, but she should otherwise be healthy and strong. Seeing the sire may be more difficult, especially if he does not live at the same premises. If that is the case, ask to see photographs of him. Check that all the puppies have been properly wormed. All puppies have worms and it is most important that they have all received the correct treatment.

Look for a friendly and active puppy. One that readily comes to you will be well worth taking a closer look at. This applies whether you are looking for a pet and companion or a show Stafford. Make sure the puppy you choose is strong and healthy, and is not shy and reserved. It is particularly well worth while spending some time with the most friendly, active and lively puppies in the litter. Take note of the temperament of

Buying your Staffordshire Bull Terrier Puppy

the mother. This, together with her response to people, will give an indication of how well the litter has been brought up and socialized.

When examining your chosen puppy, take note of any constructional faults you may find. Look for sound and blocky substance, with the definite 'chunky' feel of solid construction. From the side he should give the impression that he is standing in an imaginary square, and there should be no suggestion of an overlong appearance. The limbs should be well boned and substantially structured, and the feet should be neatly formed without any splaying of the toes. The front legs should be well boned, and there should be adequate width between them. The elbows should be well tucked in at the sides, with no tendency to protrude outwards.

Examine the tail by running your fingers along its length. It should be straight from root to tip. There should be no evidence of curling and it should be free of bumpy gristle formation.

Gently open the mouth and examine the baby teeth. A badly undershot bite will not improve as the puppy matures. Examine the lower jaw for any indication of thrusting outward as this could well indicate the development of an undershot bite formation. The lower incisor teeth should not be crowded together but spaced apart in a straight line across the front of the mouth.

At this stage the foreface should be short. Both skull and muzzle should be blocky, deeply

Typical young dog pup at five weeks.

A seven-week-old dog puppy.

A seven-week-old bitch puppy.

Buying your Staffordshire Bull Terrier Puppy

formed and powerful. The eyes should be well spaced apart in a broad skull. In a narrow skull the eyes will be closer together. Ears are difficult to assess properly in a puppy. It is only as the head grows that the final shape and development of the ears will be revealed. Avoid ears that are erect, and carefully consider semi-erect ears in a young puppy, especially if you are intending to show the puppy.

Lastly, ask if you can watch the puppy running around freely. Although he will be immature, you can learn a lot from watching him move. It may also indicate potential conformation problems. Most importantly, it will allow you to see how well the puppy conforms to the characteristics and temperament of a true Staffordshire Bull Terrier.

When you have completed your examination of the litter, and chosen your new puppy, the next step is to finalize the arrangements with the breeder and agree a time for the puppy to be collected. The most exciting aspect of the whole business is about to commence: bringing your new puppy home for the first time.

Siblings at play.

4 THE NEW PUPPY

Happy in the new home.

Careful preparations must be made before introducing your puppy into his new home environment. This ensures the best possible start to the relationship between the puppy and his new family. Once the time has been settled for the collection of the puppy, it is most important that everything is arranged before the transfer of ownership takes place. Sensible management throughout the whole of the dog's life will be of great benefit to all concerned. Preparation is the key. The guidelines set out in this chapter are intended to help with the decisions that new owners must make at each stage of the adventure.

BEFORE THE PUPPY ARRIVES

Some important arrangements need to be made before the puppy arrives in his new home. The following points cover the essentials.

Carefully choose where the puppy will be living, eating and sleeping. If he is to thrive and develop confidently, his place should be one that is easily accessible, warm and away from draughts, and well lit, and he must have easy access to the chosen toileting area. In any rooms the puppy can access, be sure to unplug electrical appliances when not in use and remove any dangling cables. Also remove any small objects that could be accidentally swallowed or may cause choking. There will, of course, be times when your Stafford will be left on his own during the day, but this is easier if he has a special place to go where he feels safe. Take this into account when choosing the place where he will be living. Always keep in mind that your Stafford will crave

A puppy safe and comfortable in his crate.

47

The New Puppy

human company above everything else. It is far better for your puppy to live and develop in the company of the family and any other pets than to be kept away out of sight somewhere on the premises for long periods of time.

The puppy will require somewhere comfortable to sleep, preferably in an exclusive den of his own to which he can retire undisturbed whenever he wants. If you choose to buy him a pet bed, select a tough one of hardy construction, preferably one with rounded corners that can be cleaned and maintained easily. Line it with machine-washable and comfortable synthetic fleece material. Avoid soft and comfortable dog beds as young puppies will chew them to piece in no time!

It is recommended that you purchase a purpose-built dog crate for your new puppy, ideally one that will be big enough even when he is fully grown. Again, line it with comfortable washable blankets. Leave him alone when he is in his den and he will quickly realize that it is his own personal space where he can escape the perhaps unwanted attentions of young children or other family pets. No matter what activity is going on, it will provide a secure place for the puppy. Leave the door open so he can go in and out as he pleases. At night he can sleep here uninterrupted, even possibly with the door open. The crate can also be the ideal place for the puppy to have his meals without the uninvited attentions of any other family pets.

For the owners, a crate can prove to be very beneficial. The readily accessible and removable base trays are easy to clean, making it easier to manage a puppy before he is properly housetrained. The puppy will soon learn to accept that the door can be closed when the owners leave the area or go out of the premises. This is an easy way to ensure that furniture and fittings remained unchewed in their absence! For portability, dog crates can be easily dismantled. Many hotels will accept dogs in their bedrooms if they are in a crate. Crates can also protect the upholstery in a vehicle, and for show people crates are an invaluable asset during their travels.

The only downside to the dog crate is that uncaring owners sometimes subject their dogs to long periods of incarceration with the door closed. Staffords generally accept their circumstances, but they will only fully enjoy life and thrive when they are able to be with their owners.

A puppy enjoying the freedom in a secure garden.

Check the security of your premises. Even the youngest puppies have an obsessive desire to explore the remotest parts of their territory. Do make sure there are no holes in fences or gaps through boundaries that can be exploited. Swimming pools and ponds must be made securely out of bounds – a young Stafford would definitely not be able to resist the temptation, and the outcome might be tragic. All means of entry and exit from the property should be checked, and locks and bolts examined to ensure your puppy will be perfectly safe wherever he is on the property. Staffords do get stolen, and your property needs to be as secure as possible to prevent this happening. Always remember that a puppy's conception of what is clean and what is dirty is very different from that of a human being. Make sure there are no 'obnoxious' areas, such as accessible compost heaps or areas for rubbish that can be exploited. Exposed garden fertilizers and weedkillers must certainly be removed, as must any poisonous plants.

Food for the puppy will be required from the outset. Check with the breeder regarding what food and in what quantity the puppy will be fed prior to collection. Invariably you will receive this information together with a puppy menu, but it is sensible to have a supply of the right food already at home before the puppy's arrival. All puppies must be wormed. Find out from the breeder what wormers have already been administered to your puppy, and when the next dose is due. This information is important for your vet on the puppy's first appointment.

Ensure that you have food and water bowls ready for the new arrival. This equipment is readily available from pet stores. Buy easily cleanable sorts that cannot be damaged by chewing. If you can, get non slip bowls that cannot easily be tipped over or moved around. Should you have decided to purchase a dog crate, water bowls can be attached to the inside of the crate.

For the puppy's first night try to obtain a stone hot-water bottle that can be well wrapped up in heavy towelling or a similar material. The puppy will appreciate the comforting warmth of this, as he will be missing the close contact with his mother and litter mates. Rubber hot water bottles must never be used for obvious reasons. A ticking clock can be placed by the side of the puppy's bed for the first few nights. This replicates the heartbeats of his mother and litter mates and can sometimes help the puppy to relax and sleep.

Stock up with essentials such as disinfectant and canine odour sprays to ensure a clean and healthy environment. Your puppy will also need plenty of bedding, preferably machine-washable. Vet bedding which can be supplied by your vet or most good pet shops is an ideal choice. Make sure you have all you need before the puppy arrives.

Make an appointment with the veterinary surgeon of your choice for an initial health examination of your puppy. This is necessary to ensure you have indeed purchased a fit and healthy Stafford. Arrange this appointment in advance of bringing the puppy home for the first time.

On an administrative note, it is important that you understand the arrangements for your puppy to be registered with the Kennel Club as a pedigree Stafford. Without exception, the only person who can register your puppy is the Kennel Club-registered owner of the puppy's mother. In almost all circumstances this will be the breeder you are dealing with, but it is best to have this confirmed. Registration can take place at any time during the first twelve months from date of birth. (After that time registration can still be done but it becomes a very expensive option and cannot happen if the breeder for any reason refuses to oblige or cannot be located.) Most responsible breeders will have registered your puppy's litter in time for you to receive the registration document at the time of collection.

At the time of registration the registered keeper has the option to include a choice of two endorsements: firstly, a restriction on any future offspring (progeny) of the puppy; and secondly the prevention of the issue of an export pedigree. You must be aware of, and have agreed to, any such endorsements before registration takes place. Having them removed at a later date will

Settled and comfortable at home.

The New Puppy

require the full written consent of the initial registered keeper to be sent to the Kennel Club.

Your puppy's registration certificate will contain his unique registration number, together with his own and his sire and dam's details. On the reverse the registered keeper will have signed the transfer declaration and handed it over to you for completion. To complete the transfer, you need to sign the declaration, fill in your details and send the document, with the required remittance, to the Kennel Club. A new registration certificate will then be issued and sent to you. Congratulations! You are now the new registered keeper of a pedigree Staffordshire Bull Terrier puppy.

THE BIG DAY

It's an exciting time for you, but remember that your puppy may not feel the same! It is a very big change in his young life.

The breeder may be able to provide suitable materials in case the puppy suffers from travel sickness during the journey, but it's safer to go equipped with your own. As far as you can, try to prevent the puppy looking out of the windows on the journey home as this can bring on sickness. Placing the puppy in a comfortable spot below window level can help.

When you collect your puppy, you should also receive his registration certificate (if he has already been registered with the Kennel Club) and the necessary paperwork to complete the transfer to you, plus a copy of his pedigree. This can be in any form the breeder chooses. Once the puppy is registered in your name, you will be able to obtain a formal Kennel Club pedigree at very reasonable cost, if required.

A diet sheet should be provided, clearly explaining your puppy's feeding arrangements and frequency of meals. Good breeders will usually include a small quantity of the food the puppy is accustomed to.

Before leaving with your puppy, you must come to an agreement with the breeder regarding the course of action to be taken by the parties involved should an undisclosed health defect be detected during the initial health examination by your vet. Also, you must be clear on the procedure regarding any future need for rehoming. Most reputable breeders will take back any dogs in such circumstances.

HOME AT LAST

Settling in.

Example of a useful puppy gift pack from the breeder.

So at last your puppy is home. Don't expect too much: most likely he will be confused and stressed from the journey to his new home and the separation from all he has known. With lots of attention and kindness any anxiety will soon be overcome. Let him meet his new family, and introduce him to his new surroundings, which he will quickly get used to. Put him down and let him have a run round. Go with him, and gently encourage him to explore with words of praise as he discovers his new world.

Staffordshire Bull Terriers are renowned for their love of children, but if you have children in the home, they must be taught from the start that he is not to be treated like a toy. Too often, excited young children pick up a young puppy only to drop him, sometimes causing severe damage to the puppy's limbs. If they are sensibly and firmly instructed, children will quickly begin to respect the puppy and learn just how far they can go in their games with him.

It is important to introduce the new puppy to other family pets. Only very rarely will a family dog or cat harm a young puppy. Dogs will usually sort themselves out quite quickly, and the family dog – provided his nose is not put out of joint by any obvious preferential treatment for the newcomer – will quickly learn to accept the puppy and they will become loyal friends and companions. This is especially the case if the puppy is of the opposite sex. Cats and dogs have a natural dislike for each other, and a little more time and patience may be required before they can form a bond of friendship. A small puppy will usually cause no problems and simply wants to play, but the cat may clearly show his dislike for what he sees as an unwelcome intruder. Great care should be taken to ensure the cat's sharp claws do not inflict any real damage on the youngster. Patience is required, but eventually the cat, realizing that his position in the home is not going to be challenged, will invariably pal up with the puppy. Staffords and cats living in the same home often become the very best of friends and companions. Correctly taught, the puppy will also quickly learn to respect other family pets such as rabbits or hamsters, and will not harass them or treat them as toys. Always keep the puppy's food separate from that of any other family pet, and well away from temptation. Carelessness in this regard can lead to unnecessary and avoidable problems.

The golden rule with puppies is to start as you mean to go on. This means that the training and socialization of your puppy starts as soon as you bring him home. It requires kindness, gentle persistence and patience, but never any form of corporal punishment. It is great fun, of course, and a source of constant amusement to join in with the entertaining antics of a young puppy doing

My new friend has arrived.

The New Puppy

just about anything he likes. But remember, if you let him get away with it as a puppy, with only the minimum of correction and training, then he will think it's still acceptable when he is a powerful full-grown adult. By all means, love him, play with him and cherish the time when he is very young, but always try to channel his behaviour in the right direction so he will become an adult you can be proud of.

TOILET TRAINING

Persistence and patience are required from the moment the puppy arrives. Allocate an area for his normal toilet functions and gently persuade him to use it. Choose a word of command such as 'toilet!' or 'outside!' and always use that word at the appropriate moment. The puppy will soon learn what it means. Never smack him or scold him if he gets it wrong. A very young puppy in particular will have no idea why you are cross with him. Persist with the quiet routine and it will all come right with time. Puppies may not appear to respond at first but all the time they are learning and identifying with their routine. When he eventually starts getting it right, he will look forward to any praise or fuss he receives.

Ready to obey the 'toilet' command.

Before he goes to bed at night, every time he wakes during the day and after each of his meals, take him to the toilet area and use the word to encourage him to go in the correct area. As he grows, you will find your Stafford will become a very clean dog and all the early training will have been well worthwhile.

THE FIRST NIGHT

After all the excitement and new experiences of the first day, the time will soon come for the puppy to spend his first night in his new home. Gently place him in his new bed and make him comfortable, ideally with a well-wrapped hot water bottle to lie against, and with a ticking

At the end of a long day.

clock nearby. After all the stress and excitement of the day he will probably be tired and will easily fall asleep. But be prepared for the sleep not to last for very long. And when he wakes up, he may feel lonely and somewhat bewildered, at which point he will start to cry for attention. Unless he becomes very distressed or frightened, and is clearly not going to stop crying, it is best in the long run just to be patient and wait for him to go back to sleep. If you go to comfort him whenever he cries, he will quickly learn that crying will bring the attention he wants. Whatever you decide to do, resist any temptation to have him on the bed with you. You could well regret that decision as the puppy will not want to sleep anywhere else after that. After a few disturbed nights most Stafford puppies settle down as they become familiar with the new routine.

FEEDING

The breeder should have provided you with details of the puppy's feeding regime up to the time you collected him. A small supply of food may also have been given to help ensure he settles in properly in his new environment. Four meals a day are recommended for the young puppy. Two of the meals should be protein based and two of them milk or dairy based. An appropriate puppy menu is given below.

PUPPY MENU

8.00am	Weetabix or similar with clear honey. Add a mix of milk and warm water.
12 noon	Puppy complete food with minced beef or chicken.
4.00pm	Same as at 12 noon.
8.00pm	Same as at 8.00am.

A bowl of fresh water must be available at all times.

You may decide to change the puppy's diet to a food of your choice. There are many complete puppy foods on the market. Select one of proven good quality, ideally containing no artificial colours or additives. Cheap foods will not necessarily provide the best nutrition for strong, healthy and vigorous development. To avoid any tummy upsets, always mix the old food with the new, and gradually introduce the new food over a few days. This will help the puppy adjust to the new diet. At about fourteen weeks your puppy will start to lose interest in milk meals. Gradually reduce the number of meals your puppy has, until by the age of about nine months he is having only one meal a day.

VISITING THE VET

The first visit to your vet is most important. Your vet will examine the puppy and discuss with you his current health status. This should be sufficient for you to be sure that his health and overall conformation are as you expected.

Inform the vet about what worming treatments the puppy has had to date. He will be able to advise you about future worming requirements. Health vaccinations are not required for very young puppies, as they retain a natural immunity acquired from their mother. The vet will advise on the correct time for the vaccinations. They usually take place in two stages, and your vet will be able to tell you how long after completion of the course you should wait before taking your puppy out and about.

Your puppy may already have been identification microchipped by the breeder. If not, your vet will be able to make the necessary arrangements. It is strongly advised that your puppy is microchipped.

Other benefits can arise from this first visit to the vet. Take the opportunity for some socialization by introducing your puppy to staff members such as veterinary nurses and receptionists.

SOCIALIZATION – THE EARLY MONTHS

Correct socialization, nutritious feeding and regular exercise are the keys to owning a healthy and contented Staffordshire Bull Terrier you can be proud of. The process is much easier if your puppy has come from a breeder who has socialized him properly during those vitally important early weeks. Ideally your Stafford should be brimming with confidence from the very start in the company and security of his new family. From the very beginning talk calmly and gently to him. When he does something wrong or needs correction, always use the word 'No!', spoken calmly but firmly. Although at first you will be dealing with an apparently scatterbrained youngster, do persist and he will eventually learn the meaning of this command. Of course, when he does something right, then enthusiastically heap praise on him and let him know that you are pleased with

The New Puppy

A young puppy happy and confident.

Lead training your puppy is the responsible way to present your puppy to the outside world.

him. Spend time with your puppy and handle and fuss him as much as you can. This will help with his confidence and bonding. Always remember that you have a Stafford: he is not a lap dog, nor when he is older will he appreciate being picked up.

After he has had his vaccinations, you can begin to take your puppy out. Take every opportunity to introduce him to friends and agreeable strangers. Walk him among crowds, but be careful to avoid people who are not comfortable with dogs. Allow friendly people to come up and fuss him. He will very much relish any attention because Staffords simply love people, and especially children. When in public places, however, always be aware of other dogs in the vicinity: Staffords are not always as well disposed towards unfamiliar dogs as they are to people.

PLAY

Play is a crucial part of growing up. With ever-increasing confidence, your new puppy will soon be sniffing out and exploring everything within the bounds of his territory. His sharp little baby teeth will certainly target any shoes or slippers left lying around. Anything that can be grabbed will be played with and quite possibly ripped up and destroyed, so be careful to keep anything that is valuable well away from him. A stair gate can be useful to prevent him venturing upstairs. Open fireplaces should always have suitable fireguards and any exposed electrical wiring should be well concealed from attention.

Provide a number of dog toys for the puppy to play with. This will help to prevent damage to items in your home and will give him something play with in bed at night and when he is alone. Choose the toys with care. Even very young Staffords have powerful jaws and teeth. Soft toys are likely to be ripped up and destroyed in minutes and can prove to be dangerous if parts are swallowed. Hard 'indestructible' toys such as kongs

The New Puppy

Looking for mischief.

help the development of soundness in the body and strength in the feet. It also helps to keep the claws short.

For a young puppy, avoid toys and games that promote excessive stretching, leaping and jumping as such activities can result in often severe damage to young tendons and ligaments. Be aware that your Stafford may get excited almost to the point of frenzy if a game becomes too exciting. This can cause trouble, especially when other dogs are involved. Watch your puppy's eyes and if they appear glazed over, then stop the game at that point and allow him to calm down.

Children in the home should be taught to respect the puppy's privacy, and to leave him undisturbed when the games are over and he flops down to sleep. During sleep he will be developing and growing and should be left alone until he awakes normally. In turn, the puppy must learn that the children are not his litter mates and must not be subjected to rough-and-tumble and biting games.

are best; they will keep the puppy busy and help to further develop his already strong jaws. There are many forms of dog tugs and pulls available, and most puppies love to participate in a grip, tug and pull game with their owners. Such toys play an important part in exercising the young puppy. Played on hard surfaces, vigorous games will do much to

Teaching the very young puppy the 'No!' command.

The New Puppy

In the early stages sometimes 'No!' may not be enough to stop a young puppy having fun!

There will inevitably be occasions when the magic command 'No!' is required. You may not want your energetic young puppy jumping up onto the furniture and chairs, tugging at or swinging from your curtains, or joyfully scrambling up the legs of visitors and people he meets. These canine 'asbo' offences need to be corrected as early as possible; if they are allowed to become habitual, they will become very difficult to control as the puppy grows. So for these and any other anti-social behaviours, no matter how amusing they may appear to be in a very young puppy, start straight away with 'No!' every time. That is all that is required, and your puppy will soon learn what it means.

Check the puppy's health daily. He will probably enjoy the attention and handling that goes with this, and it's a good idea to incorporate some gentle grooming into the session. Staffords are one of the shortest coated dog breeds and their coat requires little attention and no trimming. You can use a soft brush or a grooming glove. If the coat is groomed regularly, there will be little need for bathing your Stafford. The natural oils in the coat should keep it in good condition. Of course, if he has rolled in something obnoxious then a bath is certainly necessary. Be sure to use a

Safe and sound.

shampoo formulated for dogs; human shampoo is not suitable.

Introduce a routine for those times when your puppy has to be left alone. If he has a dog crate as his den, and he is to be shut in it, then before closing the door make a fuss of him and give him a special treat or chew that will help him settle.

Never show favouritism between family pets. If you have another dog, always make sure you treat them equally to prevent jealousy. If you make a fuss of one, or give him a treat, you must do the same for the other. A young puppy may not be jealous of an older dog, but it will be a different story as the puppy grows up. Likewise, any preferential treatment shown to the puppy can cause resentment and jealousy if the older dog feels he has been pushed aside.

COLLARS

A very young puppy will not be ready to go for walks, but it is most important that he starts to wear a collar as soon as possible. An inexpensive puppy collar is all that is necessary. It should be adjustable to allow for growth. You may find you get through several collars before he can wear a proper adult collar. Some puppies take to wearing a collar without any problems, but many don't and will do all they can to remove it. Persist and encourage with praise until the puppy accepts it. Choose one that is neither too narrow nor too wide, and avoid heavy cumbersome ones. Adjust it so that it fits comfortably. Take care that the collar is not too loose: a puppy running around and catching such a collar on a protruding object can lead to disastrous results.

When your puppy is happy to wear his collar, start to introduce the lead. As with the collar, some Stafford puppies will start to walk on the lead without any problems, but most will protest vigorously from the word go and do all they can to resist this new restriction on their freedom. Persist with patience and encouragement. Take the puppy outside, preferably on a hard surface, and gently but determinedly persuade him to move with you for a few minutes at each session. A small dog treat and much praise when things start to go right will eventually do the trick. An

A puppy in the garden and ready to play.

older family dog walking on a lead in front of the puppy can be a great help as the puppy will follow his pal. Once the skill of walking on a lead is learned, there should be little to worry about when he is old enough to be taken out for his first walks outside your premises. An identity disk giving your contact details must be attached to the collar. Should your puppy escape or go missing, this will be an invaluable aid in helping to get him home safely and quickly. The microchip offers the ultimate identification method but requires your puppy to be taken to be scanned.

For older puppies and adult Staffords various types of lead are available. Make sure that the lead you select is comfortable and offers sufficient control when necessary. Choke chains or leads of any description or design should be avoided as there is a risk of strangulation, and they do not give much control in an emergency. An extending lead is a useful option, especially for puppies. Although somewhat cumbersome to hold, it will allow your Stafford a degree of freedom to run around, but you still have control and can haul him in when necessary. For the adult Stafford a leather lead of manageable length and sufficient width is recommended. A harness offers certain advantages. All Staffords, no matter how well trained, have a desire to push forward with great enthusiasm. A harness will eliminate chafing of the fur on the neck and any choking caused by a collar in these circumstances. A harness will not, however, allow as much control as a sound collar in an emergency. Perhaps the best option is to use a harness in combination with a separate collar that you can clip on to if necessary.

CARS

Most Staffords love to be taken out in the car. They enjoy looking out of the windows (closed of course) and seeing everything passing by. Some do get car sick, especially on long journeys. Always be prepared for this with a young puppy and have cleaning-up materials available. Do not scold the puppy, as this will only inhibit his recovery and hinder your efforts to overcome the problem, and try not to make a big issue of the situation. Instead, calmly reassure him. As the puppy grows up, take him on lots of short journeys and make the whole experience fun for him and he will soon get over the problem and wholeheartedly welcome any opportunity to jump in the car

Never leave him alone in the car for more than a few minutes. Staffords do get stolen, so be warned. Always ensure there is adequate ventilation. Dogs can perspire only through their pads and their tongue, and overheating can be fatal. A high temperature sustainable by a human being can be lethal to a dog.

TEETHING

Your young puppy will be equipped with a set of small sharp teeth that will serve him well for the first months of life. Get into the habit of regularly checking his mouth and teeth. It is a fairly simple

Oh, those sharp teeth!

task with a puppy, but it's a different matter with a reluctant adult so getting your puppy used to it will help him to accept his mouth being examined when he is older.

When your puppy reaches the age of about four to five months, his baby teeth will start to drop out and be replaced with new adult teeth. It is normal for the mouth to be painful and his gums will be swollen. You can help him by providing sturdy things to chew, such as the chews obtainable from pet shops. During teething you must check that there are no complications and that the emerging new dentition is coming through correctly and not being inhibited by baby teeth that remain in the gums. Generally there is nothing to worry about and the transition will proceed perfectly well. Sometimes, however, the baby teeth are reluctant to come out and one or more of the gums will contain both a baby and an adult tooth. This is usually only a temporary problem but if you are concerned, have his mouth examined by your vet. Do not attempt to extract the old baby teeth by any means.

One problem that can occasionally arise in Staffordshire Bull Terriers during this debilitating and painful teething time is a temporary lowering of a puppy's resistance. One of the symptoms is coat loss. It shows up as patches of baldness and in extreme cases can be quite worrying. The bald patches vary in size, most often appearing on the head, flanks and legs. The skin sometimes looks inflamed and sore but more commonly shows up as areas of grey. Staffords affected by such unsightly patches do not appear to be in any way concerned about the condition. Vets will often diagnose a form of mange, with small mites in evidence. In severe cases, a veterinary consultation is advisable. In most cases the problem clears up quite naturally, the mites vanish and the fur grows back by the time the new teeth are well developed at about nine months of age.

Various treatments have been suggested, but they tend to be very expensive. A sensible diet occasionally containing some oily fish products such as sardines or pilchards does seem to help the process of recovery. Applying benzyl benzoate – a milk-like liquid obtained from a pharmacy – can also help to cool down any inflammation of the affected areas.

EXERCISE AND THE YOUNG PUPPY

A healthy diet and the correct amount of regular exercise will keep a Staffordshire Bull Terrier in optimum condition. Be careful not to overdo the exercise with a very young puppy. For the first few weeks all he needs is plenty of opportunities for running and playing on some hard surfaces. By

Something to chew with my puppy teeth.

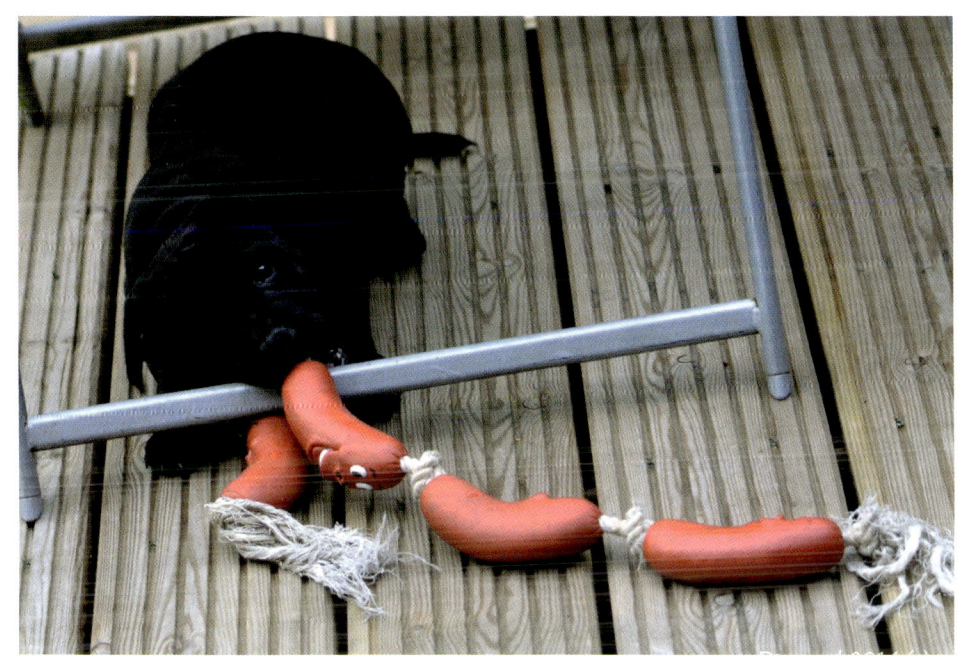

The New Puppy

Happy and healthy.

the time he has completed his initial vaccinations and can go out, short walks a couple of times daily will suffice. Your Stafford, being a Stafford, will gladly dash along to the point of exhaustion, but you must not allow him to do too much as it can cause damage to developing ligaments and tendons.

As the puppy grows and strengthens, the walks can be gradually increased. About two miles a day at the age of six months should be enough to keep him in good condition. After the age of nine months you can take him as far as he wants to go. There is no better exercise to ensure a fit and hard condition in an adult Stafford than regular walks on hard surfaces.

'I'm off!'

5 OWNING AN OLDER OR RESCUE DOG

Oldies but goodies. Gus and Giff were my first two Staffords.

CHOOSING AN OLDER DOG

Making the decision to buy a Staffordshire Bull Terrier puppy is an exciting prospect, but some people would prefer to give a home to an older dog. Whatever the reasons for the choice, there are always good opportunities available to them.

There are several advantages in choosing an older dog rather than a puppy. The older dog, for example, is likely to be house-trained, especially if he has ever lived in a house. Not everyone wants to go through the rigours of house-training a new puppy. He should also be over the chewing stage that puppies go through as they are teething and growing.

An older dog may already be able to demonstrate good behaviour and his capability of being a very good companion. This can be an important issue for a prospective new owner who may be physically impaired or in poor health and lacks the confidence to start at the beginning with training a puppy. He may already be trained to walk nicely on the lead and behave properly in public with people and other animals. He may already be familiar with basic commands such as 'No!', 'Stay!', 'Leave!' and so on. These are all practical points – but it may be, of course, that an older dog simply appeals to a prospective new owner.

If the intention is to show, there are certain advantages in obtaining an older dog. For instance, the opportunity may arise to purchase a dog with a proven show record and plenty of potential showing ability. This is a much safer bet than buying a puppy which may never achieve anything in the show ring. Bear in mind, though, that a proven dog that has already obtained high honours in the show ring but is still young

A much-loved old girl.

61

Owning an Older or Rescue Dog

enough to be successfully shown will be a very expensive purchase. Another option may be to purchase a proven sire of quality puppies. Again, this may be an expensive acquisition but such a dog is more likely to produce quality progeny than an as-yet-unproven puppy.

An older ex-show Stafford.

Perhaps the best time to obtain an older dog is when he is around one or two years old and has plenty of life ahead to be enjoyed.

ELDERLY DOGS

Such dogs may perhaps require a new home due to a bereavement or because their owner can no longer care for them. Elderly dogs often require special care and attention, which their new owner will need to be aware of.

- There can in old age be a reduction in the dog's mobility that can lead to health-inhibiting weight gain. Older dogs are much more prone to gain weight than younger ones, especially if they have been neutered or spayed.
- The maintenance of a sensible weight is a most important factor in ensuring good health. An elderly Stafford that is overweight will likely have mobility problems because of the strain on his bones, ligaments and tendons, as well as difficulties with his respiratory system, heart and other internal organs. It is inexcusable not to do all that can be done to prevent an old dog becoming obese.
- Maintaining an old dog's health and general well-being can be achieved by paying strict attention to his food requirements. Your veterinary surgeon will always be there to advise on this if necessary. Generally, a healthy dog only needs to be fed once a day to satisfy his dietary needs, but for an older dog it may be better to divide his food into two portions, fed in the morning and evening. This puts less wear and tear on his digestive system. Various high-quality specially prepared diets are available for older dogs.

An old girl happy to be out and about.

Owning an Older or Rescue Dog

Enjoying the field.

- The exercise regime for a dog of advanced years must be handled with care. Due to his very nature a Stafford will want to keep on going as if still a youngster. The owner must be sensible and never allow an 'oldie' to overstretch himself. Sensible exercise as long as he is capable and fit enough is one thing, but allowing him to harm himself is another.
- A worming routine should continue during the dog's advanced years but due care must be taken if he is unwell. A vet can advise you.
- Old dogs often have bad breath, and it may indicate a problem that needs veterinary attention. It is often caused by insufficient or neglected cleaning of his teeth. If he is not accustomed to it, an 'oldie' may not take kindly to having his teeth brushed. Special chews that need to be properly chewed up and cannot just be quickly swallowed can help. For dogs that are missing some teeth, a softer type of chew is more appropriate.
- Very old dogs may suffer from failing eyesight. They seem to adapt well to the problem, and even to their owners may not appear to be suffering unduly. Should his eyesight deteriorate or even fail, the dog will still be capable of leading as happy and relatively normal life as long as he is well cared for. Do not move the furniture around in your home, as this will confuse him and he will lose his bearings.
- Problems with his toilet, and particularly with his water works, often occur with a dog of advanced years. He cannot help it and should never be scolded for his occasional mishaps. Any punishment would be totally non-effective and would simply cause unnecessary confusion and stress for the dog.
- It is most important for a dog of very advanced years that he is allowed his dignity and an undisturbed place in the home, without being pushed around or out of place by boisterous children or younger animals.
- The time will inevitably come when it becomes necessary to say goodbye. When an 'oldie' has reached the state where he is no longer able to maintain his life with dignity and freedom from pain, it is time to prevent any further suffering and see that he is gently put to his final rest.

Maybe old but very happy.

REASONS FOR REHOMING

Before making the decision to become the owner of an older dog, always determine exactly why he has become available for rehoming. There are

Owning an Older or Rescue Dog

many reasons why an owner may want or need to find a new home for a Stafford. Some of the most common are as follows:

- a domestic breakdown means the dog can no longer be sufficiently cared for;
- a family is going to live or work abroad and cannot take their dog with them;
- the family is moving home and cannot have dogs in their new premises;
- due to a genuine change of circumstances, perhaps unexpected unemployment or the like, an owner can no longer give the dog a good home;
- a keen show-goer may have run a Stafford on, only to find he has developed a fault that disqualifies him from showing successfully;
- breeders may want to find a good home for a sound and healthy dog that has been sold and returned because he simply didn't fit in with his new family; or
- breeders may want a good home for a young bitch who has whelped a litter of puppies but will no longer be used for breeding.

In any other circumstances, you are strongly advised to look into the real reason why the dog is up for rehoming. Perhaps he is dangerously or destructively out of control. Factors such as lack of proper training, poor home environment, ill treatment and even sometimes total frustration due to neglect can all play a part in creating a dog with difficulties. A dislike of small children may be given as a reason. Certainly it is very unusual for a Stafford to be guilty of this and it needs looking in to. It may be that the dog is simply attempting to protect himself from unbearable teasing by young children.

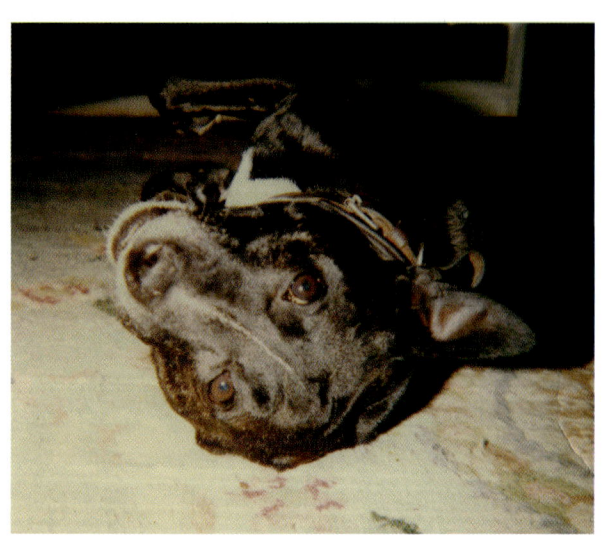

Be very wary if you are told that a dog needs a new home because he bites without warning. This is most unusual behaviour in a Stafford, and, if it is true, then you should consider very carefully the risks involved in rehoming such a dog. Sometimes dogs are put up for rehoming because they are not clean in the home and the owner is just passing the problem on to someone else. The Stafford is a very clean dog by nature, and the problem may have been caused by inadequate toilet training or anxiety due to an unsuitable environment. An owner may want to rehome a dog because the neighbours have complained about barking. This usually happens when the dog is left on his own for long periods without proper attention.

Unscrupulous breeders may wish to pass on a dog that cannot procreate or a bitch that cannot conceive. This will not always be given as a reason for rehoming. If you are hoping to breed from your rescue dog, you need to do some research into this to avoid any future disappointment. Likewise, an uncaring owner may wish to pass on a dog that has developed health problems. This can turn out to be very expensive, so make sure you have a health check done before purchasing any dog.

In any event, it is best to take the dog on approval for an agreed period before a transfer of ownership is completed.

More than forty years ago – an old Stafford enjoying life in a loving home.

Owning an Older or Rescue Dog

A GOOD CHOICE?

There are various reasons why a Staffordshire Bull Terrier might be in need of a new home. Fortunately for these dogs, there are many people who want to share their homes with a pet and a rescue Stafford often makes an ideal choice. They are very special dogs with a reputation for outstanding character and temperament, and an admirable record for loyalty and devotion to all members of a family, young children and elderly alike.

Some Staffordshire Bull Terriers find themselves desperately in need of new homes, but seldom through any fault of their own. In many cases breakdowns in family relationships or bereavements result in them having to be rehomed. Others are the result of irresponsible over-breeding by the uncaring. Some are dumped or abandoned, and wander the streets as strays until picked up by the authorities or members of the public and put into rescue. It is not unheard of for owners to turn out a dog because it is inconvenient and they just want to get rid of him without particularly caring where he ends up. Such people should never have a dog in the first place. This is not to say that all Staffords that end up in rescue are unloved. Sometimes, especially in the case of bereavement or illness, an owner may simply be unable to look after the pet properly and there is nowhere else to turn for help. But sadly, the rescue authorities come across all too many cases of neglect, malnutrition (even starvation) and outrageous cruelty to Staffords. No matter the level of abuse such victims have endured, once safely in rescue they will be treated with enormous care, often at great expense, to help them overcome whatever trauma and injuries, whether psychological or physical, they have suffered. They will receive veterinary attention, be spayed or neutered (if not already) and generally prepared for rehoming with an approved new owner.

Three of the Staffords rescued by Northern Staffordshire Bull Terrier Rescue.

These dogs are crying out for a new start in life with owners they can love and be devoted to. A visit to any rescue kennels will clearly demonstrate this. But taking on a rescue Stafford is not easy. A prospective owner must expect to be thoroughly checked out as to their suitability to take on a rescue dog and a home visit will be arranged in order to ensure that the accommodation and environment will be satisfactory for the dog. In return, every Stafford will be carefully assessed prior to going to his new home. His character and temperament will be carefully matched to a prospective new owner, taking especial care where young children are present in a household. Rescue Staffords are there because they have fallen on hard times. No one wants to see that happen to them again.

A prospective rescue owner should ensure that the dog has been fully checked over by a qualified veterinary surgeon and received any necessary medical attention, including neutering where appropriate. Full vaccinations must have been carried out, and an identity microchip implanted.

> **RESCUE STAFFORD WALKS**
>
> To see a long trail of Staffordshire Bull Terriers with their devoted owners and families all together on one of their special organized weekend walks through beautiful countryside is a never-to-be-forgotten experience. They are of all ages, shapes and sizes, but they all have something in common: all are rescue Staffords owned by people who would never consider any other choice of dog!

There are many dedicated rescue organizations for dogs that are in need of new homes. The Kennel Club each year produces a Dog Rescue Directory which lists both general rescue organizations that deal with all breeds and breed-specific rescue groups. The Directory is intended to assist in the rescue of stray and unwanted dogs. It is not designed to replace the purchase of puppies from responsible breeders, but is a resource intended to help people who want to rehome an abandoned dog or who need to find a suitable home for their own dog. The Kennel Club endeavours to ensure that organizations included in the Rescue Directory are genuine, but has no control over the way in which they are run since they are not bound by Kennel Club regulations.

Below is a list of the Stafford rescue organizations included in the current (2015) Kennel Club Rescue Directory.

Leicestershire Staffordshire Bull Terrier Rescue
Mrs Norma Vann (Co-ordinator)
Leicestershire
01662 606365
www.sbtrescue.com

Leicestershire Staffordshire Bull Terrier Rescue
Mrs Helen Treece
Leicestershire
01332 557630
www.sbtrescue.com

North Eastern Staffordshire Bull Terrier Rescue
Mrs A. Hubery
Co. Durham
01388 606000
Nozac.hubery@googlemail.com
www.northeastStaffordrescue.org

Northern Ireland Staffordshire Bull Terrier Rescue
Julie Jenkins
Northern Ireland
07563 368 589
sbtjulie@googlemail.com
nisbtr.co.uk

Northern Staffordshire Bull Terrier Rescue
Anna Murray
Scottish Borders
07747 831293/4
www.sbtrescue.org.uk

Northern Staffordshire Bull Terrier Rescue
Mr B. Whittall (Co-ordinator)
Cumbria
01539 530245
07977 061125
bob@sbtrescue.org.uk
www.sbtrescue.org.uk

Scottish Staffordshire Bull Terrier Rescue
Fiona Hay
Edinburgh
07989 650693
www.Staffordrescuescotland.co.uk

Scottish Staffordshire Bull Terrier Rescue
Mr Stuart Evans (Secretary/Trustee)
Moray
07973 916724
www.Staffordrescuescotland.co.uk

Scottish Staffordshire Bull Terrier Rescue
Shona McCann (Trustee)
Aberdeen & Grampian area
07725 632232
www.Staffordrescuescotland.co.uk

Scottish Staffordshire Bull Terrier Rescue
Mrs Kay Hamilton (Trustee/Chairperson)
Scotland
07923 546993
07775 875993
kay@westerlea.org.uk
www.Staffordrescuescotland.co.uk

Scottish Staffordshire Bull Terrier Rescue
Anne McWilliam
Glasgow
07477 600572
www.Staffordrescuescotland.co.uk

Scottish Staffordshire Bull Terrier Rescue
Alison Senior (Trustee/Treasurer)
Scotland
07775 875993
www.Staffordrescuescotland.co.uk

Scottish Staffordshire Bull Terrier Rescue
Linda Ross
North of Scotland, Highlands and Islands & Moray
07816 454162
www.Staffordrescuescotland.co.uk

Scottish Staffordshire Bull Terrier Rescue
Jessica Dalgleish
Scotland
07786 450100
www.Staffordrescuescotland.co.uk

Scottish Staffordshire Bull Terrier Rescue
Shirley Duncan (Trustee)
North of Scotland, Highlands and Islands & Moray
01463 741018
Staffordrescue@btinternet.com
www.Staffordrescuescotland.co.uk

Scottish Staffordshire Bull Terrier Rescue
Sharon Hamilton (Trustee)
Lothian & Scottish Borders
07870 538944
www.Staffordrescuescotland.co.uk

South Eastern Counties Staffordshire Bull Terrier Rescue
John and Gwen Laker
Kent
01227 471647
john.staffrescue@vfast.co.uk

Staffordshire Bull Terrier Rescue
Mrs Barbara Green
Lancashire
01204 573942
Barbara.sbtrescue@btinternet.com

Staffordshire Rescue Scotland
Rescue Co-ordinator
Scotland
07594 897338
07544 001099
saveaStafford@yahoo.co.uk
www.staffordshirerescuescotland.org.uk

Owning an Older or Rescue Dog

BRINGING HOME THE OLDER OR RESCUE DOG

Much of the advice given in the chapter on bringing home a new puppy will apply equally to the older or rescue dog, but there are some significant differences and much depends on the dog's circumstances. If he is not too old, and has come from a good home, he should be able to adapt to the change in his circumstances relatively easily. His new owners will generally have the advantage of knowing from the outset – from the information provided by his previous owners – of what is needed to help him adapt and settle down comfortably. For an elderly Stafford extra care must be taken to ensure his welfare. For example, he may need a special diet containing a lower protein content. Increasing his fluid consumption, perhaps by adding water to his meals, will help to keep him in good condition and protect his kidneys. Your veterinary surgeon will be able to advise on sensible calorie-controlled diets to avoid weight gain. An elderly Stafford needs exercise, but not as much as when he was young. Care needs to be taken to ensure he does enough, but not too much.

Two other potential problems are bad teeth and arthritis. The older dog may well be suffering from bad breath caused by tartar, decayed teeth or both. These conditions will require the attention of a veterinary surgeon. Arthritis in old age is a not uncommon problem, and can cause the older dog considerable pain. Your vet will be able to supply medicines and supplements to help relieve the condition.

Sometimes, especially in the case of abandoned dogs, little is known about the dog. Great care, dedication and patience will be required to help build his confidence and trust. Some may have been treated most cruelly and have suffered terrible trauma. The new owner must be prepared to be endlessly patient and dedicated in giving such a dog a new start. Retraining may be necessary, but it will all be worthwhile in the end – for at the end of the journey there will be a healthy and happy Staffordshire Bull Terrier who loves and trusts his owners.

A very contented older dog.

6 HEALTH, WELFARE AND NUTRITION

So much energy!

The aim of all responsible Stafford owners must be to ensure soundness, good health and a long and happy life for their dogs. This aim should be the same for all Staffords, whether young or old, dog or bitch. This chapter will consider various aspects of health, welfare and nutrition.

When you take your puppy to the vet for the first time, there are four areas that should be discussed: vaccinations; microchipping (if not already done by the breeder); worming; and flea and tick treatments.

VACCINATIONS

Various diseases, some of them with potentially very serious consequences, can affect your puppy so it is vital that you have him vaccinated as soon as possible after collection from the breeder. The first injections may already have been given by the breeder's own vet, especially if you have bought a slightly older puppy, in which case you will be given an inoculation certificate to be handed to your own vet. A puppy must be fully immunized before being allowed out to make contact with other dogs outside the home. He must not be taken out for walks or allowed to sniff or play anywhere where other dogs have access until the vaccinations have been given time to take effect. This is usually a week or two after the second injection. After that time your puppy will be free to mix with other dogs and can be taken anywhere with you.

For the older dog, much depends on the information and any documentation that came with him. Your vet will determine any vaccinations that are necessary at the initial health appointment.

The initial vaccinations consist of modified forms of infection that do not cause illness in a dog but activate his immune system and stimulate the formation of antibodies. In this way

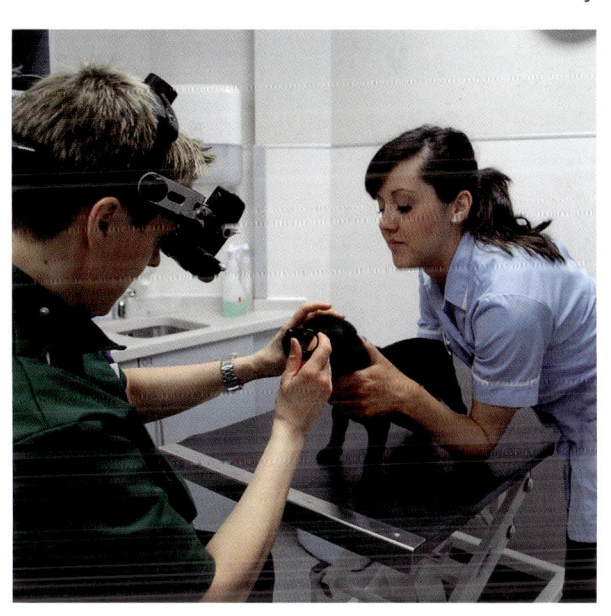

Visit to the vet for a health check.

Health, Welfare and Nutrition

they protect your Stafford against various lethal and debilitating contagious conditions, some of which are described below:

Canine distemper is a contagious and highly infectious serious illness that affects the dog's respiratory and nervous systems. There is no known cure but it is preventable by vaccination.

Canine hepatitis is a rapid-onset and potentially fatal liver infection. Dogs that recover from hepatitis can pass on the infection in their urine for many months afterwards.

Leptospirosis is a bacterial disease that often affects the liver and kidneys. It is acquired through contact with urine passed by infected rats, foxes and other forms of wildlife. It can also be passed from dog to dog through infected urine.

Canine parvovirus is an acute and highly contagious viral infection that can be spread from dog to dog and results in a life-threatening illness. Much more common in puppies than in adult dogs, it can cause vomiting, abdominal pain and blood-flecked diarrhoea. Affected dogs quickly become thin, weak and dehydrated. This disease can kill a dog within twenty-four hours of infection.

Parainfluenza virus is a highly contagious respiratory condition associated with kennel cough – an unpleasant condition resulting in coughing and sneezing. Affected dogs should be kept well away from show grounds or any other public places until completely free of the condition. Initial vaccinations may now include protection against parainfluenza.

Vaccinations are essential for your Stafford. Some of the diseases they are vaccinated against are potentially life-threatening. Even if the dog survives, there may be irreparable damage to his vital organs such as the heart, liver and kidneys, and this may require long-term medical treatment. Whatever else you do, make sure you get your Stafford vaccinated! Your vet will be able to advise you about the frequency of booster vaccinations. Be aware that adverse effects may result from over-vaccination of your Stafford, so keep a record. This will also be useful if you need to place him in boarding kennels for whatever reason, as a current vaccination certificate will be required.

MICROCHIPPING

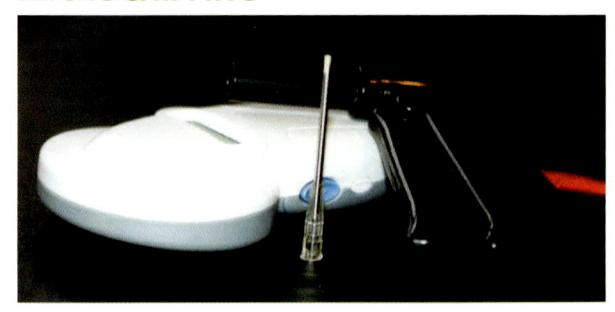

Microchipping equipment.

From April 2016 it will be compulsory for all puppies to be microchipped. It is absolutely essential that you have your Stafford microchipped, and your vet can do this for you if it has not already been done. Often it is done at the same time as the initial vaccinations. Always ensure you keep the microchip records safely filed.

The insertion of a single and permanent microchip implant into the fold of loose skin between the shoulder blades of the puppy is a simple process. The implant is about the size of a grain of rice, and the insertion is normally completed in a moment with the puppy remaining largely unaware of it. The microchip is designed to last for the dog's lifetime and should remain permanently at the point of insertion. Each microchip has a unique identification number that can be read using detectors designed for the purpose; appropriate authorities and veterinary practices in all areas have such a reader. This will enable the owner of a lost dog to be quickly contacted.

WORMING

On your initial health visit with your Stafford, take on board the advice of your veterinarian

Health, Welfare and Nutrition

regarding a lifetime worming plan. All dogs have worms, with puppies being most at risk. Responsible breeders will have started worming their puppies at two weeks of age, with regular treatments being given until the puppies are sold. Worming should continue throughout the lifetime of your Stafford, whether puppy or older dog. Breeding bitches may have special requirements.

Roundworms are intestinal parasites and are common in dogs. They can grow very long and live on nutrients absorbed from the dog's food. If infected, your dog will not thrive. Puppies can be infected with the larvae while still in their mother's uterus, and can also take in larvae from their mother's milk.

Tapeworms are large and very unpleasant. Sections of them can sometimes be detected in the faeces of infected dogs. They require an intermediate host such as raw meat or fleas to complete their life circle.

There should be no doubt of the seriousness of a worm infestation in your Stafford. Preventative treatment should be a top priority. Both roundworms and tapeworms must be catered for in any worming programme and an effective, safe, combined treatment will be available from your vet.

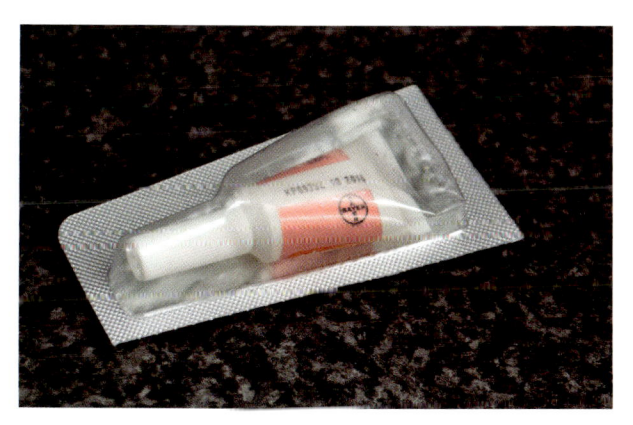

Pipette of flea/worming treatment.

FLEA AND TICK TREATMENTS

Most dogs will suffer from flea infestations at some times during their life. Fleas can be brought into your premises by your Stafford from just about anywhere and at any time of year. So flea treatment should go on all year round. Fleas and flea dirt can easily be detected in the short coat of a Stafford by parting areas of the fur and looking on the skin. There are many forms of treatment available to deal with the problem.

Ticks are most unpleasant and more seasonal than fleas. They can be picked up in long grass in parks and gardens. To help protect your dog, during hot weather try to avoid woodland areas or moorland where sheep or cattle have been grazed. Ticks anchor themselves to the skin and use their mouthparts to suck blood, eventually swelling up to the size of a pea. If you find a tick on your dog, do not attempt to pull it off. There are special tick removers that will remove them safely, but seek expert advice if you are not sure how to go about it.

There are certain spot-on preparations that will kill both fleas and ticks. Your vet will be able to advise you on their use at your initial appointment.

Fit, healthy and happy.

Observing and adopting all these recommendations will ensure an excellent start on the road to establishing a good and healthy relationship with a newly acquired Staffordshire Bull Terrier, but there is much more to consider. It is advisable to adopt a regular daily routine, adapting it to suit either an elderly dog or a young puppy at appropriate times. This will help to ensure that

Health, Welfare and Nutrition

he thrives and remains sound and healthy. Your routine should cover the following points:

- **Appearance and behaviour.** Check that your Stafford looks to be in sound and healthy condition. He should always be eager to play games and join in family activities and walks. Check for any obvious cause if he does not enthusiastically respond in the way you expect from him.

'Look at my lovely teeth'. A young puppy.

- **Coat.** Regularly observe the state of your Stafford's coat. All dogs shed their coats and the Stafford is no exception. Such shedding should not be excessive, however, and there should be no evident signs of scurf. There will be a 'doggy' smell about his coat, but this is normal and in no way unpleasant. Certainly there should be no evidence of excessive irritation or scratching, which would require careful attention. A quick daily brushing with either a special brush or a glove designed for the purpose should be included in your routine. The coat of a Stafford should 'gleam' with health, and a good diet and correct exercise will help with this. Check for evidence of parasites such as fleas and treat as necessary.

- **Teeth.** In a puppy, the transition from baby to adult or permanent teeth should be completed by the age of nine months. Adult teeth should be brushed and checked daily and any signs of plaque or tartar promptly dealt with. Left unchecked, tartar will build up on the teeth and will eventually lead to tooth decay, resulting in bad breath and discomfort for your dog. The teeth will become discoloured if not brushed regularly. Regular brushing will greatly help in maintaining your Stafford's mouth in a healthy state throughout his whole life. It is not an easy task to get him to accept his teeth being brushed, but making it fun, with lots of praise and small rewards, will do much to help. Special brushes and dog toothpastes are available for the purpose. Persistence will pay off in helping to prevent unsightly and unhealthy mouth conditions. Dental chews are also available that will help with teeth cleaning. Cleaning the teeth is an important aspect of care and must not be neglected. Patience and regularity are the keys to success.

An older Stafford showing clean dentition.

- **Ears.** Regular inspection of your Stafford's ears is advised. The presence of a brown or smelly discharge should be dealt with promptly with a trip to the vet. Constant shaking of the head and scratching of the ears can indicate irritation that needs to be attended to. A daily check will help immensely.

Health, Welfare and Nutrition

Eyes should be bright and shiny.

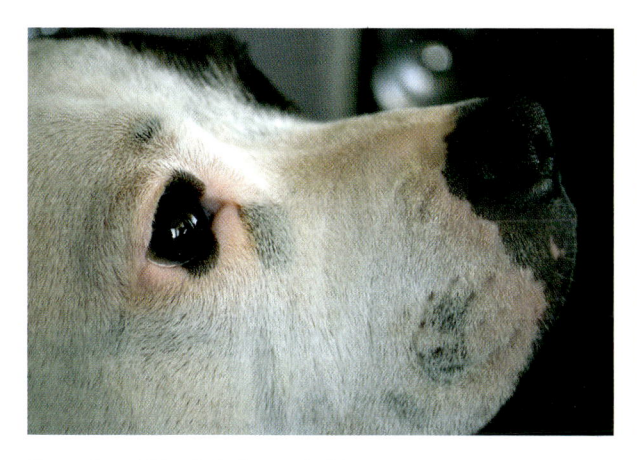

Nail clippers.

- **Eyes and nose.** A quick daily check is all that is necessary to see that the eyes are bright, clear and alert. Any weeping should be looked into to determine the cause of the problem. The nose should always be moist, cold and shiny. A warm dry nose often indicates illness.
- **Claws.** The claws should not be broken, nor too long. Your Stafford should not suffer from over-long claws if he is regularly exercised over hard surfaces. The shorter the claws, the better for him, and ideally they should end at ground level. Should they need trimming, either through lack of correct exercise or ill health, be sure to use good-quality nail clippers. Your Stafford, with patience, will become used to regular trimming. Little and often is the recommendation, and only the very tip of each claw should be removed each time. The blood vessel to each claw runs through the nail, and if accidentally cut, it will bleed profusely and cause much pain. As the claw gets shorter, so the blood supply will recede and a little more can be cut. It may be a tedious procedure perhaps, but it is necessary if the claws have grown too long. The alternative is to ask your veterinary surgeon to do the job for you. Although it may be expensive, at least the job will be done properly.

The dew claws, which are located on the inside of the front pasterns, are best left alone but sometimes they curve and grow inwards, and may even penetrate the skin. In this case, your veterinary surgeon can advise you.

Garden play is exercise too.

Health, Welfare and Nutrition

Feeding time!

- **Stools and Urination.** Check daily that your Stafford performs his regular toilet functions as normally as possible. Stools should be passed regularly, and a correct diet should ensure no evidence of diarrhoea or constipation problems. Any evidence of blood in the urine should be investigated immediately to determine the cause. Male Staffords urinate more frequently than bitches in order to mark their territories. This is normal.
- **Weight.** A close eye should be kept on your Stafford's weight. He should be in fit and hard condition throughout his lifetime. Too many owners allow their Staffords to gain weight. This does not do them any favours, no matter how contented they may appear. The key to weight control lies in a correct diet, restricted snacks and treats and the proper amount of exercise.
- **Exercise.** Your Stafford requires daily exercise. He will feel the full benefit of it, and so will you! There should be no reason to worry about over-exercising him. A fit and healthy adult Stafford will cheerfully go as far as you can manage.
- **Feeding.** Feed your Stafford at regular times every day. The bewildering array of foods available will be discussed in the next section.

NUTRITION

A correct and nutritious diet, combined with regular exercise, will do more than anything else to determine your Stafford's health, fitness and general appearance. He should appear lean and muscular, and carry no excess weight. When you run your hands along the sides of an adult Stafford, you should be able to feel his ribs; if not, then he is too fat. Deliberately starving a Stafford in the mistaken belief that this will make him look lean and fit is cruel and cannot possibly be recommended. His health will deteriorate badly from such treatment. In the old days dogs would have been stripped down immediately prior to a

Health, Welfare and Nutrition

fight in order to minimize their weight but such practices have no place in today's world.

Generally, throughout his adult life, as long as your Stafford looks well and healthy, there is no reason to change the chosen diet. Do bear in mind, however, that the better the diet, the better the dog. Certainly this applies to his overall health and general condition. Sometimes, however, it is a matter of trial and error to find a food that suits the dog to his own and your satisfaction. Hopefully, all will go right for the dog from the start. Usually this is so, as the Stafford is a very healthy and rugged breed. As your puppy grows and develops into an adult, you must be prepared to change the formulation of his diet. Likewise, for the sake of his health you must be ready to make changes to his diet as he ages, if he is suffering from certain illnesses or conditions, or if he becomes fat and has a weight maintenance problem.

A rapidly growing puppy requires a very different diet from an adult or elderly Stafford. You do not necessarily have to change a diet that has proved ideal for the puppy, but simply move on to the adult or senior formulations of the same diet as appropriate. Just as with humans, dogs' nutritional requirements change at different stages of their life. For example, a young puppy will

Good quality food is important for all Staffords, young and old.

Fresh water must always be accessible.

Health, Welfare and Nutrition

require a diet that will support his rapid growth, but such a diet would not meet the needs of an elderly dog. As a rough guide, a Stafford up to eighteen months of age should be fed puppy food, from eighteen months to seven years adult food and from seven years onwards senior food.

Again as a rough guide, a young puppy should be fed four times daily until he reaches three months of age, when it can be reduced to three meals a day. At six months of age he should be fed on two larger meals, and at twelve months he should be fed as an adult on one main meal daily. There are many excellent ranges of quality dog foods available, and the appropriate quantities to feed will be displayed on the packaging.

A good quality diet is essential for a puppy but resist any temptation to over-feed him. This will be of no benefit to him and may even cause abnormal growth patterns. Advances in the science and modern technology of dog food has led to a growing belief that a young puppy – from as early as four weeks of age – can be put straight onto a 'growth formula diet'.

An older dog, from the age of nine or ten years and onwards, has different requirements. Do make sure that his food is rich in high fibre and is highly palatable. It should contain increased amounts of fatty acids and vitamins, and a reduced amount of protein. A low-calorie diet will aid the conversion of body fat into energy. Your veterinary surgeon will be able to advise you in choosing a low-calorie diet for your elderly Stafford.

Always ensure there is plenty of fresh water available, not just at meal times. Do not give milk to an adult dog as he will not be able to properly digest the lactose contained in it. The digestive system of a newly born puppy is designed to digest his mother's milk but this will progressively change as the puppy grows older.

A raw knuckle bone is a great treat.

As an aid to digestion, it may be helpful to divide the adult Stafford's daily meal into two portions and feed him one in the morning and the other in the evening. Do not make the mistake of feeding over-large portions if you choose to feed your Stafford this way.

Should it become necessary for you to change your Stafford's diet, do not introduce the new food all at once. This will usually result in an upset to his system or even a complete refusal to eat the new food. Gradual change over a period of a few days is the best way. The following pattern of change is to be recommended:

Days 1–2: 75 per cent of original diet/25 per cent of new diet.
Days 3–4: 50 per cent of original diet/50 per cent of new diet.
Days 5–6: 25 per cent of original diet/75 per cent of new diet.
Day 7 onwards: 100 per cent of new diet.

Enjoying a healthy diet.

Health, Welfare and Nutrition

It is unusual for a healthy Stafford to be a fussy eater. There are exceptions, however, and if he is reluctant to take the new food, try feeding it as a treat by hand with lots of praise until he gets used to it. If your Stafford has been used to eating wet food and you change to a dry kibble-type food, always moisten it with some warm water until he is used to the new texture.

Complete dry dog food.

Wet food.

Whatever diet you consider best for your Staffordshire Bull Terrier, it is important to ensure it includes the correct balance of ingredients required to sustain him in optimum health and condition. There is a bewildering choice of foodstuffs available from which you can make your choice. You may also wish to choose alternative diet. Dogs are omnivorous, but a suitable diet for a Stafford should include substantial amounts of good-quality animal proteins and fats as this will best suit his digestive system. Try to avoid any foods containing a large proportion of carbohydrates.

The fundamental ingredients of any dog food will be listed on the packaging. They include:

- **Proteins.** These organic compounds are an essential part of a dog's food: indeed, without the inclusion of protein in his diet, your Stafford would not survive. A dog's ability to digest protein varies; for example, he can absorb proteins more easily from meat or fish products than he can from vegetable sources. Feeding too high a level of vegetable protein can cause bowel upsets. If you choose to feed a vegetarian diet, your dog will require supplements such as Vitamin D.
- **Carbohydrates.** These are energy-producing compounds. They include starches, cellulose and sugars. Fresh meat and fish do not contain carbohydrates, so if you have chosen a meat- or fish-based diet, be sure to include additions such as potatoes or rice to provide the necessary proportion of carbohydrate.
- **Fats.** Fats are the best sources of energy. In the form of fatty acids, they are an essential part of a dog's diet and play a vital role in his well-being. A deficiency can be the cause of health problems such as nervousness and skin disorders. Nearly all of the fat content in a dog's food will be digested. With the high level of energy produced, he will not need to digest so much protein, which reduces the strain on his kidneys and liver.
- **Fibre.** Sufficient roughage in the diet aids digestion and helps to reduce bowel disorders such as flatulence and diarrhoea. It can also

Health, Welfare and Nutrition

aid the absorption of toxins – poisonous by-products of digestion – and thus can ease the strain on the dog's liver. There are other advantages. For example, increasing the amount of fibre in the diet of an overweight Stafford will help to satisfy his appetite without increasing his weight. Fibre absorbs glucose and thus can help dogs with a diabetic condition.

- **Energy.** This is expressed in the form of calories. Your Stafford should be fed in accordance with the amount of energy required for his breed. Younger, more active dogs will possess a faster metabolic rate than older or less active dogs and will therefore require food possessing a higher energy content. Adjustments also need to be made for a lactating or pregnant bitch or a dog suffering from illness.
- **Vitamins and minerals.** The correct balance of vitamins and minerals in the diet is of vital importance, not only for the proper functioning of the body, but also for prevention of disease. Particularly important are the correct proportions of calcium and phosphate, both of which are crucial to overall development, strong bone formation and healthy teeth.

A fat Stafford is not a fit one. Overfeeding should be avoided at any time. Follow the feeding charts included on the packaging of all ready-prepared dog foods, which contain all the elements listed above in the correct proportion. Should you decide to feed your Stafford fresh or home-made food, you will need to ensure you are providing enough vitamins and minerals.

TYPES OF FOOD

Long gone are the days when an average adult Stafford's diet consisted of a pound of cooked or fresh raw meat mixed with a handful of biscuit meal, supplemented with a few vitamins and minerals. There wasn't necessarily anything wrong with that, but today there is much greater selection to choose from. Most of these foods are scientifically produced and nutritionally well balanced, providing the correct proportions of all the vital ingredients required to sustain a healthy and fit Stafford. Some can be fed without any additions whatsoever to the dog's food.

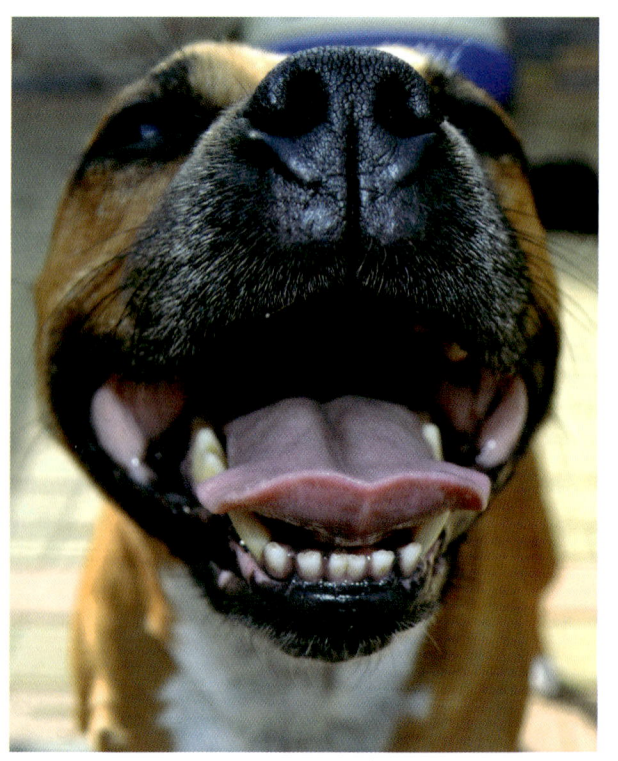

A minced raw diet, supplied frozen.

'Is it nearly dinner time?'

- **Complete dry foods in the form of kibbles.** These are commercially produced and are the most popular choice for Staffords. They generally contain meat or fish, plus grains and vegetables. Supplied in convenient packaging, they do not smell offensive, are easy to store and are generally relatively economical. Purchase prices vary according to the quality of the ingredients. These are complete foods and do not require any additions. A good-quality complete dry food provides all the protein, carbohydrates, fats, minerals and trace elements a dog needs in a highly digestible form. Precise feeding charts are available for each stage of the dog's lifetime. Many of these foods contain no artificial colouring, preservatives or flavourings, and no wheat, gluten or soya is included in their formulation.
- **Canned or wet foods.** Another excellent choice, canned foods contain all the necessary nutritional requirements, including vitamins, minerals and trace elements, for a healthy Stafford. They are mainly meat-based, often combined with vegetables or corn products. They do contain a high percentage of water and once a can is opened, the contents need to be consumed before they lose their freshness. They are usually high-quality foods and tend to be more expensive than kibbles over a period of time. Dry dog biscuits are usually mixed with canned foods, and can assist in keeping a dog's teeth clean.

  All-meat canned foods need to be fed in large amounts to provide the necessary energy required. Without the addition of fortified mixers, they will result in an unbalanced and unhealthy diet.
- **Semi-moist foods.** These are a popular method of feeding. They are highly concentrated and contain only a relatively low percentage of water, allowing for economical quantities to be fed at each meal. They are usually packaged in individual servings. Highly digestible and very palatable, these foods contain meat or fish, vegetables, cereals, fats, vitamins and minerals and provide everything necessary for a healthy and well balanced diet. They are gently cooked, which helps to retain natural vitamins.
- **Home prepared diets.** For those with a sound knowledge of the requirements for a healthy diet, it is possible to formulate a healthy diet utilizing fresh ingredients to suit your dog. Provided the correct dietary requirements for a healthy Stafford are fully taken into consideration, there can be advantages to processing and cooking your own dog's food. It is vital to ensure the required levels of proteins, carbohydrates, fats, minerals, vitamins and trace elements are present to avoid any risk of your dog being deprived of some of the important nutrients. This is especially important for puppies, where any dietary deficiency can result in abnormal growth and can have a significant adverse impact on the puppy's optimum development.

  Unless prepared expertly, many homemade diets lack the necessary elements, often because the owners do not fully appreciate the correct balance of ingredients required. If you choose to make your own, it is recommended that you follow the expert advice given in the various recipe books available on the subject.

  An increasingly popular example of a raw food diet is the 'Barf' diet, 60–80 per cent of which is made up of raw meaty bones containing about 50 per cent of the meat from, for example, chicken neck, back and wings. The remainder is made up from offal, meat, eggs, dairy foods, fruit and vegetables. As with any form of diet, there are arguments for and against diets such as 'Barf'. Much depends on the dog's acceptance or otherwise of the diet, although given that dogs evolved over countless years on a natural raw diet, it seems logical that such a diet is an available option.
- **Frozen.** Packaged in loaf form, these contain a very high percentage of meat ingredients. They are most palatable but do need to be supplemented with good-quality dog mixer biscuits to ensure a well balanced diet.
- **Leftovers.** Leftover food from the dinner table has no place in the feeding of your Stafford, particularly not for developing puppies.

Health, Welfare and Nutrition

It can cause a nutritional imbalance, potential development issues and a tendency towards unwanted weight gain. If you give your young Stafford titbits he will soon learn to be present whenever food is about. Resist his appeals!

- **Raw meat and biscuit.** This was a popular type of diet in the days before the availability of modern scientifically prepared foods, but it required additives and supplements to provide all the elements of a balanced diet. If you choose to adopt such a diet, take care not to give your dog too many vitamins as this can cause damage to his bones and joints.
- **Organic diets.** Some dog food manufacturers now supply organic foods. Mostly in dry form, they contain organically raised meat and organically grown maize, vegetables and rice. All organic dog food must carry a label of certification on the packaging.
- **Bones.** A good meaty bone will give your Stafford many hours of enjoyment and provide a great way to exercise his jaws and clean his teeth. Avoid chicken bones and any cooked bones that may splinter in his powerful jaws. If bone splinters are swallowed they can cause severe internal damage, often resulting in an expensive operation. The best choices are large knuckles or marrow bones. The latter will also provide your dog with vitamins and calcium from the marrow.

Finally, do not be tempted to continuously change the diet of your Staffordshire Bull Terrier in a determined quest to ensure you are giving him the best. If he is strong, healthy and happy with his diet, then just leave him alone to enjoy it.

7 TRAINING THE STAFFORDSHIRE BULL TERRIER

Most Staffords eagerly respond to training.

A well trained Staffordshire Bull Terrier is a pleasure to own, and teaching him to fit in with the family should be an exciting – if challenging – experience. The most important aspect of training is that it must be enjoyable and rewarding for both dog and owner. Above everything else it should be fun.

An eight-week-old puppy possesses needle-sharp little teeth, with which he will want to bite and tear up everything, and the concentration span of a gnat! With infinite patience, and praise when he does it right, he will make progress as he learns that correct behaviour will win for him a delicious treat and lots of enthusiastic praise from the boss.

Every Stafford puppy needs to be trained so that he settles into a happy and harmonious relationship with his owners. Just imagine what it would be like if your dog was allowed to do whatever he wanted to do. Without knowing, he would be misbehaving – and as a result constantly punished and shouted at. Without training, he wouldn't understand what was acceptable behaviour and what was not. What should be a happy and rewarding time with his owners would be chaotic and stressful. Worse, an untrained Stafford will lack respect for his boss and pack leader. Dogs always look to their pack leader to be in control and will only be bewildered by inconsistent requirements they do not fully comprehend. This is what sensible training and correct socialization is all about. Make it the aim from the very start of the relationship to ensure that your Stafford is well socialized and properly trained and you will soon be well on the way to developing that special bond of confidence and respect between you and your dog.

The type of training required will very much depend on the expectations of the owners and how they require their Stafford to fit in with their lifestyle. Always remember that puppies, just like small children, need guidance, motiva-

'Enough said!'

Training the Staffordshire Bull Terrier

tion and mental stimulation. Well thought-out training will take these requirements fully into consideration. Many owners want a Stafford as a pet and companion, and are not interested in training him to compete at dog shows or take part in other canine activities such as agility competitions. For the pet Stafford training to conform to the social requirements of his home will be sufficient.

Preparing your Stafford for the show ring will be fully dealt with in Chapter 10, but it will suffice here to say that even dogs who are destined to compete at the highest level in the show ring must begin with the same training as the pet or companion dog. They will, of course, then need to be further trained in order to successfully compete in the show ring.

Great benefits can be derived from the socializing and training facilities offered by the many dog training clubs around the country. Plenty of help and advice is also on hand. As well as training the dogs for the show ring, these clubs offer the opportunity for invaluable interaction with many other dogs of all breeds. In addition, Staffordshire Bull Terrier Clubs run specific training classes for Staffords.

Meeting at the training club.

Taking your Stafford to a training class should not be problematical. Take him along when he is as young as possible and at that age he will quickly adapt to all the attention and company. Staffords like to please, and will respond admirably to the challenge! In some cases Stafford owners go along to train and socialize their dog, only to become convinced that their pet is very capable of doing well in the show ring or in other competitive activities. This may open doors to a whole new adventure!

TREATS

Treats are very important to your Stafford, and successful training largely depends on the value of the treat to persuade him to concentrate and do what is required. A dog's sense of smell is far more powerful than any of his other senses, and certainly it is far more powerful than that of a human. This fact should be fully utilized. Find a treat that is totally irresistible to him and you can guarantee his undivided attention. Make sure you have plenty of his favourite treats available

Training clubs can be great fun.

The temptation of it all.

whenever training is in progress. These treats should only be given during training.

It really doesn't matter what the treat is, as long it is something the dog really likes. Meaty is best, and it should not contain too much biscuit, which is high in sugar content. Don't select something too large and chewy – a Stafford chomping away while the judge is attempting to examine his mouth will not be helpful. The ideal treat should be small, and easily accessible. Remember to offer treats from the palm of the hand as treats held in the fingertips can result in a painful nip from an over-zealous dog.

Only reward your Stafford when he does something right. If he doesn't get it right, he doesn't get the treat. Simple, isn't it? Giving treats as rewards is the key to training a Stafford successfully, and in as happy and fun manner as possible.

TRAINING FOR THE YOUNG PUPPY

- When a young puppy comes into his new home, you need to make decisions from the start about where he can and cannot go. If you don't want him to jump on the furniture or on the beds, start training him right away that these items are out of bounds. If you want your puppy banned from a particular room in the home, a firmly voiced 'No!' will soon do the trick. He must learn that he is not going to be the pack-leader in the home, and to do this make sure that you initiate the behaviour required. You must call the shots and be the one that sets the pattern of social behaviour to determine the order of things. Do not let the irresistible little rascal elevate himself above his place on the social ladder. Even the sweetest, most submissive puppy will try to do this as his confidence grows. Unless taught otherwise, the puppy will seek any way he can to arrange the order of social interaction within his family to suit himself. Start the training as soon as you can, as it is much harder to do once the incorrect pattern of behaviour has been established.

- Toilet training is one of the first matters to concentrate on (*see* Chapter 4). Where the puppy is going to live will largely determine how to proceed. A location as close as possible to outside access is clearly the best solution, but is not always possible. Staffords are very adaptable, and given the right care they will happily thrive in most forms of accommodation.

Is this where I go?

Consistent use of a command such as 'Outside' or 'Toilet' is recommended. After every meal, and whenever he wakes from sleep, gently carry your puppy to the allotted area and give the command word. He will soon go. When he does, give him lots of praise and fuss, and maybe a treat. He will soon begin to associate the action with the command. There will be accidents, of course, and laying down newspaper around the den will help in the early stages. Do not punish him for accidents. When trained properly, Staffords very quickly learn to be clean dogs. Persistence will pay off, and result in a clean, house-trained puppy.

For Staffords living in accommodation with limited or no outside access, the use of disposable puppy training pads is recommended. Place one of these pads in an area which is easily accessible and familiar to the puppy. Once he has accepted it, never place the pad in another area as this will only confuse him. Whenever he wakes up and after all his meals, take him to the pad and give the command. Give him plenty of praise when he goes. There will inevitably be accidents in the early stages, but gentle persistence will be successful in the end. Used training pads must never be shared by any other pets, and should be bagged and disposed of.

- Dogs are essentially pack animals. Make it your objective right from the start that your puppy identifies you as his pack-leader. In the early stages of training motivate him by treats and toys as rewards. Never resort to any form of harsh treatment. Reward-based training is always the best way. Get the whole family to handle the puppy and fuss him all over. This will not only encourage confidence but greatly help him to find his place in the pecking order. He will soon learn what behaviours bring rewards.
- Look out for puppy parties being held locally. These are usually organized by veterinary establishments and are open to very young puppies of all breeds. Such parties are a great opportunity for your new puppy to make friends and join in the fun. But do be aware that young Staffords play 'rough', and this

Someone said 'Sit'.

Training the Staffordshire Bull Terrier

Someone said 'Stand'.

may not go down too well. Young Staffords are often considerably stronger than other puppies, and may bite just that little bit too hard, so choose his playmates with care.

- Start to train your puppy to walk on a lead around your garden as early as you can, and certainly before you take him into the outside world. This will not be easy at first as the puppy will probably object most strongly, pulling backwards, bucking, struggling and otherwise refusing to co-operate, but do persist. He will soon become used to it and can be encouraged along by holding a treat in front of his nose. Having an older dog in the home is useful here as most puppies, shown the way by the older dog, soon catch on and learn to follow. When he is old enough to be allowed out, it is a good idea for him to be accompanied by an older dog to a park or open space where the two can play and walk together on their leads. The puppy will then soon forget about any restrictions caused by his lead.

- All too soon the time comes for your puppy's first walk! By this time he should be used to a lead and collar but everything else he has ever learned will be completely forgotten in the excitement of all the new sights, smells and sounds in this new environment. You must be

Meeting a new friend.

85

patient and he will soon settle, despite this exciting new world. If available, take another dog with you and your puppy will quickly adjust in the company of a pal.
- There is nothing better for a young Stafford than to be taken out and introduced to all kinds of situations. Get him used to walks on a lead into shopping areas, along busy streets and anywhere where he will encounter new people and particularly children. He will be constantly fussed over. Encourage this as he will be learning to adapt within society. Don't allow him to leap up or be a nuisance. Many people cannot resist fussing a young happy puppy, and he will love it. So will you! Familiarity with such situations, combined with consistent training to behave properly in public, will result in a Staffordshire Bull Terrier you will be proud to own and take out.

- A young Stafford must not be taken for long walks until he is at least six months of age. It is easy to let this happen, as he will always be very enthusiastic and want to go further. But be sensible. Playing at home, combined with short walks in the park or in fields, is the order of the day. A growing puppy can all too easily be damaged physically by overdoing his exercise on long walks or engaging in strenuous activities. Once he reaches the age of about nine months this restriction can be lifted, and he will probably be capable of out-walking you any time! Always ensure that your young Stafford's collar is tightly and securely fastened. There should be just enough space between the collar and the neck for your fingers. Train him not to resist the lead as any attempt to push backwards and slip out of his collar could have disastrous consequences if he should escape onto a busy road.
- Many young Staffords suffer from car sickness. You can begin to overcome this problem by taking your young Stafford for a short ride in the family car every day. He will soon get used to these trips and start to look forward to them. Incidents of sickness usually stop quite quickly, especially if the puppy is not admonished in any way for the occasional lapse. Long trips may sometimes cause even an adult Stafford to become sick. Never scold your dog - he can't help it.

  Most Staffords quickly learn to love the car and will happily jump in and go for a ride. Be aware though, that they will often guard the car from passers-by.
- Consistency is important. Always use a simple single command word such as 'Stay!', 'Stand!', 'Sit!' or 'Heel!'. You can also use hand signals when appropriate. Provided you use them consistently, they will help to reinforce the verbal command. Deliver your commands in a firm and clear voice. Don't shout, and don't add unnecessary words. Never lose your temper if things are not going right. Any devia-

'Where are we off to today?'

A treat for a good girl.

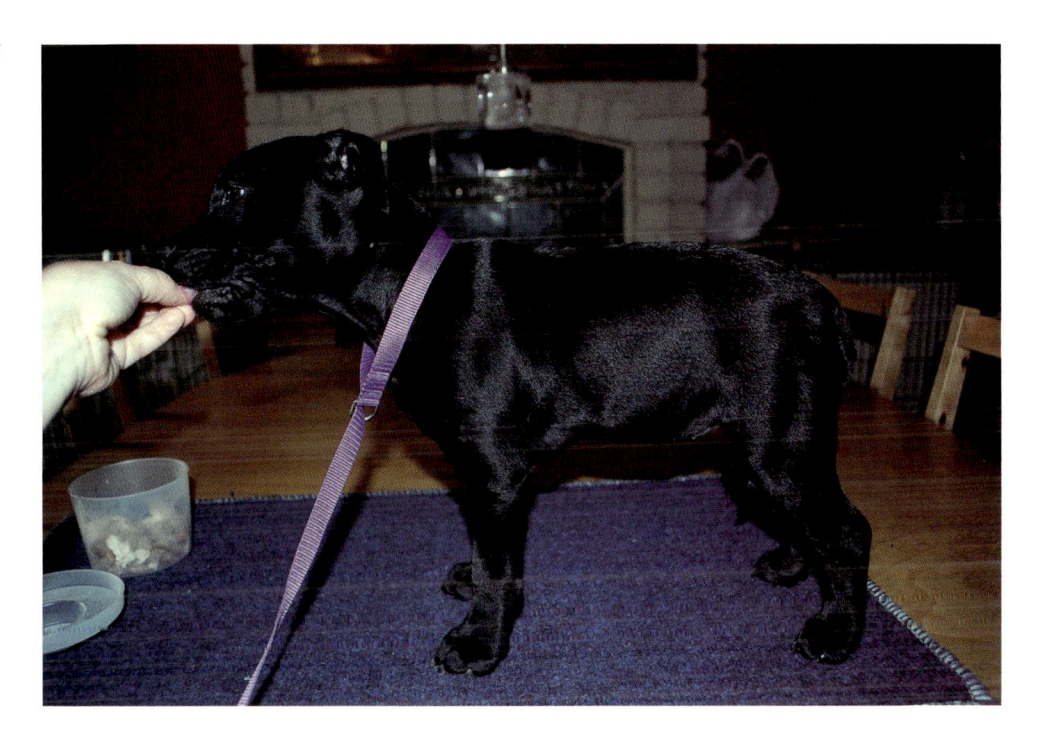

tion from your normal calmness will only be counter-productive as it will simply confuse the dog.
- Always approach every training session in a good humoured and confident manner. This will do much to encourage your Stafford to join in and enjoy the fun. Always make sure you have that treat ready. When your Stafford finds that he is rewarded for a particular behaviour or action, he will be keen to repeat it. Rewards must be given immediately so that he associates the desired action with the treat.

   With the irresistible treat already in your hand, hold your palm upwards in front of his nose and give the command 'Take!' Your Stafford will be delighted to respond. If he makes a grab for the treat, close your hand so he can't get it and resettle him. If he takes it gently, let him have it and make a big fuss of him. This shows him that you are pleased with him. This approach applies to all types of training. You may need to repeat everything time and again, especially with a young puppy. Remember that young Staffords are generally slow to mature and can be easily distracted. Always be patient and it will all fall into place sooner than you expect.
- Never reward bad behaviour with a treat. A certain amount of discipline and determination will be needed to show the young puppy that you are his pack-leader. Like a naughty child, he will push the boundaries to see how far he can go, but he really must not be allowed to get away with it. Remember that you are dealing with a young puppy, and what is required is gentle discipline in the form of good-humoured persistence. Introducing the 'Non-reward' is helpful. In other words, when your Stafford gets it wrong, he doesn't get a treat. He may get it wrong time after time but don't give in. He will be frustrated by this lack of treats and will eventually begin to experiment with his own behaviour until he finally gets that delicious treat. Gentle, friendly and continuous encouragement from you will help him, as will heaps of praise when he gets it right.
- As he gets older, and learns your commands, it will not be necessary to reward him with a treat every single time he gets it right, but always praise him. This should be enough.

Staffords are intelligent dogs and will quickly learn to be obedient without the need to be constantly rewarded.
- Punishment is *not* the opposite of reward. It is a not the case that a Stafford will effectively respond to punishment by a diminishing of undesirable behaviour. Shouting or in any way physically assaulting him will not work. The non-reward approach is much better at controlling or eliminating bad behaviour and the command 'No!', delivered firmly, is far more effective than any form of punishment.
- With a young puppy, keep the commands short. Don't do too much too soon, and always keep it simple.
- A young puppy during training will be very sensitive to variations in the tone of your voice. If you sound angry, he will react accordingly and become confused and unsure. If you are light-hearted, he will happily respond and want to join in with the fun. In any training session always use a warm, friendly and persuasive tone. This he will learn to associate with training and will confidently react accordingly. The message should be clear: never start a training session if you are anxious or angry.
- Any form of physical punishment is definitely out, particularly when you are dealing with a young puppy. As a breed, Staffordshire Bull Terriers are brave and fearless, and are almost unbelievably tolerant to pain. Yet they are frightened by loud bangs, gunshots and fireworks. They are astonishingly forgiving, even when they have been cruelly treated, but that is not to say a Stafford will retain his trust in a human who uses any sort of physical force on him. In most cases, the noise from a rolled-up newspaper slapped against the owner's leg is enough to startle a Stafford into ceasing a misbehaviour. It will not train the problem out of him: rewards and praise are always the way to train your Stafford.
- Do not train too often. Your puppy will be learning quickly and be full of the joys of life, so make sure you intersperse the training sessions with lots of play and walks. Spontaneously interrupting play can be a great time to do some training, and at the same time it will show you are in control. Then, after a short period of training, with rewards and lots of enthusiastic praise, play can continue.
- Always end a training session with something the puppy has learned to do well. Follow this up with praise and an enjoyable game. This will do much to help him realize that training is fun, especially if a treat and a game follow.

TRAINING FOR THE OLDER STAFFORD

With an older Stafford, you must gently but firmly establish from the beginning that you are the pack-leader and you set the rules – not him. The Staffordshire Bull Terrier is without doubt an enthusiastic and strong dog, and the phrase 'Act first, think later' perfectly sums up his good-natured but impulsive attitude to life. This may

A good training session ends with play time.

Training the Staffordshire Bull Terrier

'Did we do it right?'

Adapting to new training.

Fun in the park!

be endearing at times – but it can also be a nuisance. Training for a young puppy is important, but it is even more so with an adult dog who has been allowed to misbehave in the past. He may already have been trained to a degree, but you will need to adapt his training to your ways and establish the ground rules for his behaviour in your home. For instance, you may have to teach him not to jump up. When he does so, signal with your hand and firmly deliver the command 'Down!'. Look him in the eye for a moment, then on your terms, allow him to come to you for a fuss. This will start to establish the necessary chain of command. He will learn to carefully observe your body language and respectfully approach you accordingly.

The older Stafford may well need to go back to basics for his toilet requirements too, as he won't know what is expected from him at first. Staffords generally want to please, and should adapt fairly quickly to the new circumstances, provided you are positive and encouraging. Retraining in the 'command, reward and praise' manner is recommended.

Training from the outset for the older or rescue Stafford will need to take into account what he already knows, whether good or bad. It is important to find out as much as possible from his previous owners, use that knowledge and adapt it accordingly, otherwise he may have no idea what is expected from him. As he learns, never scold him for lapses. Instead, always enthusiastically encourage and reward successes as he gradually adapts to his new way of life. Make this a challenge to be enjoyed both by owner and dog. You will be going the right way to forge a mutual bond of trust and friendship.

It is an unfortunate fact that older Staffords may tend to have a history of aggression. This is not acceptable. The Stafford is a very powerful dog for his size, and any form of aggression must be brought under control firmly and swiftly. Training an older dog to instantly obey his owner's commands is of crucial importance in avoiding any potential confrontation, particularly with other dogs.

Fundamentally there are two distinct forms of aggression: aggression towards people and aggression towards dogs. All breeds of dogs will bite and some, regardless of size, have a reputation for snapping and biting at people. The Staffordshire Bull Terrier, whose Breed Standard requires him to be totally reliable, is not one of these. It is rare indeed to hear of an instance of a genuine well bred Stafford biting a person in anger. Any such act of aggression would need to be dealt with immediately and decisively. Regretfully, no amount of retraining would help in such circumstances. Fortunately, the Staffordshire Bull Terrier is one of the most reliable and affectionate breeds obtainable, with an unequalled reputation for dependability with people, and in particular with children.

In contrast, Staffords will react if another dog shows aggression. His natural instinct is to assert his dominance when faced by another dog. It is important to understand that this aggression is only directed at other dogs, and not at people. Never take it as an indication of unreliability as a family pet. Train him from the start to avoid the possible consequences of aggression involving other dogs. Many responsible Stafford owners know what it is like to have their dog safely under control on a lead, only to have another dog, running free and out of control, charge towards him. Train your Stafford to resist such confrontations by instantly obeying your command to leave the other dog. It is not worth becoming entangled in what can all too easily develop into a nasty situation. Never allow your Stafford to run free in public places in the vicinity of other dogs. No amount of training will be of help in any resulting fight involving your dog. Your Stafford off a lead and engaged in a fight with another dog would be deemed out of control, and may lead to an infringement of the Dangerous Dogs legislation.

HOW TO APPLY THE COMMANDS

Clear commands are vital training aids. From day one, teach your dog to respond to your everyday commands. With a puppy, make sure you only introduce them gradually so that you don't confuse him. You can choose your own words, but as a guide here are a few examples:

The 'Stand' command.

Stand! This one is very useful in the show ring and is used when a handler is presenting his dog for the judge to examine. It is quickly learned.

Walk! This is not an easy one at first. Staffords are strong and impulsive dogs, who like to surge forward at the commencement of a walk on a lead. Gradual persuasion and 'No!' commands will eventually prevail. Whatever you do, do something to prevent him pulling on the lead. Otherwise you may end up with very long arms and with your dog gagging and choking. Ideally your Stafford should walk calmly at your side, preferably on a loose lead and at your pace not his. 'Steady!' is another useful command to slow him down.

Training the Staffordshire Bull Terrier

Fetch! This is a good one as Staffords love to play. Your dog will quickly learn this command when you throw a ball for him. When he brings it back, you can also teach him the command 'Drop!' Some dogs will energetically co-operate for a couple of throws and then lose interest. If this happens, you'll have to fetch it yourself!

'Fetch!'

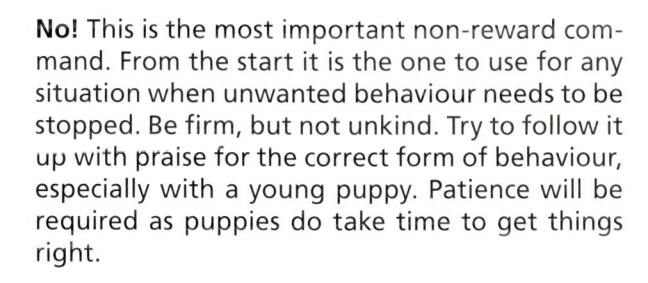

Dogs must be trained to walk properly without pulling.

No! This is the most important non-reward command. From the start it is the one to use for any situation when unwanted behaviour needs to be stopped. Be firm, but not unkind. Try to follow it up with praise for the correct form of behaviour, especially with a young puppy. Patience will be required as puppies do take time to get things right.

Down! This is another definite non-reward command. People not used to dogs will not appreciate a big Stafford jumping up at them, perhaps with muddy paws, no matter how friendly he is trying to be. This command is best taught right from the start with a young puppy.

Take! Unless taught otherwise, Staffords will be tempted to lunge forward to grab any treat you are offering him. This is not acceptable. As he does so, close your hand over the treat and don't let him have it. Settle him down again, and only let him have the treat when he takes it gently.

Watch me! This is an important training aid and can be used to get your dog's attention at the start of a training session. It will signal to him that it is time for him to concentrate. When you say the command, get and maintain eye contact for a few seconds. Reinforce your command with a treat.

Come! This is a tricky one! A Stafford running around and enjoying himself off the lead may decide to 'play deaf' and not come back to you. Do not reprimand him when he does come back, as he will associate the act of coming back with the reprimand, and next time may take even longer to return to your side.

Sit! A Stafford will sit quite naturally and will quickly learn to respond to this command. For show dogs, this is less important than the 'Stand!' command, as he needs to be standing for the judge to examine him.

Training the Staffordshire Bull Terrier

'Watch me!'

'Come!'

TRY IT!

With any new command, you will be pleasantly surprised how quickly your Stafford catches on – especially if he's likely to get a treat! Limit the use of commands to those that are relevant, and only apply them when you need to. They must be neither too repetitive nor over-administered. Unnecessary discipline or regimentation enforced on a spirited breed like the Staffordshire Bull Terrier will ultimately fail. Let your dog be a proud representative of his breed. Calmness and consistency in the use of commands will help to establish and maintain a happy and rewarding relationship between you and your Stafford.

Training the Staffordshire Bull Terrier

An attentive sit.

TRAINING AIDS

Many types of training aid are available to assist in the training of your dog, but some are more useful than others and some should be avoided altogether.

A harness can be very useful, especially for a Stafford that has any form of breathing problems. Unless taught otherwise, Staffords do tend to pull on a lead, which can result in painful choking and gagging. For some reason, they don't seem to associate this with surging forward on their lead. If your dog chokes on a conventional collar and lead, try using a harness; it will not cure the pulling problem but does relieve the pressure on the neck and throat. The harness must fit properly and securely around both shoulders and fore-legs and the dog must be comfortable in it. Be aware that a harness will not allow you the same level of control as a collar. Just in case, it is best to have a collar round your Stafford's neck at all times, to which you can clip the lead in an emergency. Brass harness decorations can be obtained for Staffords, which look attractive but may be associated in the general public's mind with certain breeds of banned dogs.

A Stafford is a very powerful dog. A choke chain will not be helpful in an emergency and is of only limited assistance as a training aid. It may be effective at stopping a Stafford from pulling, but it won't teach him not to pull in the first place.

Any type of radio-controlled shock collar is definitely to be avoided. Such gadgets are cruel and abhorrent. This should never be the way to train a proud and trusting Stafford. Electric shocks imposed in order to elicit an instant response are more likely to result in a fearful and insecure dog.

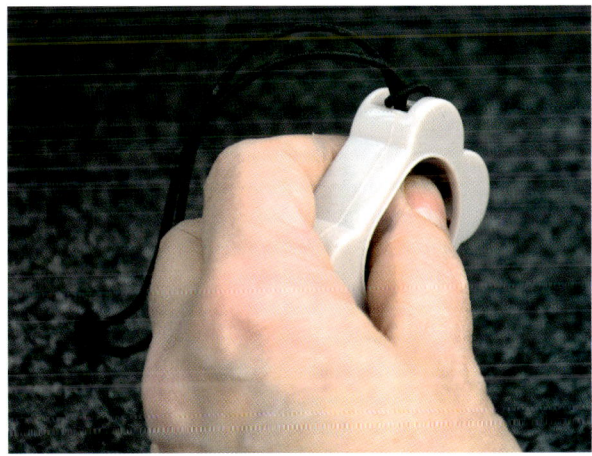

Typical clicker training aid.

Clicker trainers are excellent for teaching your Stafford, as are dog whistles designed for the purpose. Your dog will quickly learn to respond to them if you use them correctly. They make training fun, and are readily available. Staffords have an acute sense of hearing, and even if your dog has gone out of earshot of your call, he may still respond to a whistle. This can prove to be invaluable.

Training the Staffordshire Bull Terrier

AN UNDESERVED REPUTATION

Before leaving the important subject of training, it is time to focus attention on how the Staffordshire Bull Terrier is sometimes portrayed. We live in an age of prejudice, directed towards the breed by some elements of modern society. Perhaps their superficial resemblance to certain banned breeds causes mistrust in some circles, while the publicity relating to incidents of dog aggression often makes mention of the breed.

Staffords responsibly under control out in public on a walk.

All responsible owners and breeders, who know what honest and wonderfully reliable dogs Staffords are, deplore the often inaccurate representation of the breed by uninformed elements of the media. They are appalled by the damage done to the breed's image by irresponsible owners who do not train their dogs correctly and fail to take proper care of them. All Staffords are capable of responding forcefully to another dog's aggression, so it is up to their owners to ensure they can prevent potentially disastrous consequences. Proper training and socialization will enable you and your Stafford to show the breed in its true colours. We all have a part to play in this.

A litter of newborn puppies.

8 BREEDING, PREGNANCY AND WHELPING

Owners of a pedigree Staffordshire Bull Terrier bitch will need to decide whether or not to breed a litter of puppies from her. It is a major decision, and not one that should be taken lightly. There are specific Kennel Club rules regarding the registration of pedigree puppies, and there are certain circumstances in which registration is not permitted.

Assuming the Kennel Club requirements are met, another item to be taken into account is the maturity of the bitch. Is she mature enough to whelp and raise a litter of puppies successfully? No bitch should ever be mated during her first season as she would not have had time to mature sufficiently to cope with the demands of producing puppies. She must be allowed to develop – both mentally and physically – well into adulthood before having a first litter.

A young bitch will come into season every six months or so, but as she ages, so her seasons will become less frequent. Do understand that as a bitch advances in age, her heats can tend to become less frequent. If you decide to breed from an older bitch for the first time, it is advisable to seek advice from a veterinary surgeon before beginning.

Happy with mum.

Breeding, Pregnancy and Whelping

> **CONTROL OF REGISTRATIONS**
> **(© The Kennel Club Ltd. Reproduced with their permission)**
>
> (a) The General Committee may reject any application made under these regulations and may cancel or suspend any registrations or grant of a Kennel name already made and may instruct any registration to be made.
> (b) Specifically the General Committee may suspend the registration of any dog which is banned from participation in any Kennel Club licensed events as a result of a biting incident. The same provision shall apply to any registered dog which is the subject of a successful criminal or civil action in the courts as a result of a biting incident.
> (c) The General Committee will not accept an application to register a litter when:
> (1) The dam has already whelped four litters, save in exceptional circumstances and only provided the application is made prior to the mating and veterinary evidence as to the suitability of the bitch involved in the proposed whelping has been received, or
> (2) The dam has already reached the age of 8 years at the date of whelping save in exceptional circumstances and only provided the application is made prior to the mating, and the proposed dam has previously whelped at least one other registered litter and permission has been received. Any such application must be supported by veterinary evidence as to the suitability of the bitch in the proposed whelping, or
> (3) The dam was under one year old at the time of mating, or
> (4) The offspring are the result of any mating between father and daughter, mother and son or brother and sister, save in exceptional circumstances or for scientifically proven welfare reasons and permission has been received, or
> (5) The dam has already had two litters delivered by caesarean section, save for scientifically proven welfare reasons, and this only provided the application is made prior to the mating.

Remember that the offspring from an unregistered Kennel Club Staffordshire Bull Terrier (sire or dam) cannot themselves be registered as pedigree dogs. For the puppies to be registered, both sire and dam must both themselves be Kennel Club registered.

MATTERS FOR CONSIDERATION

It is well worth considering the following questions before deciding to breed from your Stafford:

- Will you keep one of the puppies, and if so, what impact will that have on the home environment?
- Have you thought about how to go about finding and vetting suitable homes for the puppies?
- Have you a suitable and secure area in the home that can be used to accommodate a bitch and her puppies?
- Do you have sufficient time available to devote to the mother during pregnancy and to the puppies from birth until they go to their new homes?
- Have you taken into account the veterinary costs involved? For example, if a caesarean section operation becomes necessary, it will not be cheap.

If you are happy that you have thought it all through and you still want to breed, then welcome to the happy adventure of bringing new life into the world! When all goes well, it is an exciting and pleasurable experience, particularly so when breeding a litter of puppies for the first

Three generations together.

time. This chapter will deal with the whole process from start to finish, but it is always recommended that you seek veterinary advice.

TYPES OF BREEDING

Clearly it is in the best interests of a responsible breeder to choose a sound and healthy stud dog, but much careful thought and planning should go into making the final selection. A clear appreciation of the most common forms of breeding may be helpful:

- **In-breeding.** This is the mating of a closely related dog and bitch in order to perpetuate desirable characteristics in their progeny. Such a mating might be father to daughter, mother to son, or brother to sister. Do take into account the Kennel Club registration requirements for puppies resulting from such a mating.

  There are many risks involved with this form of breeding. Certainly desired characteristics may well be perpetuated, but so too may be any faults, some of which may not be apparent in the first generation and are unrecognized by the breeder in either parents or ancestors. Such close breeding can result in infertility and some serious problems, particularly monorchid or cryptorchid conditions in males (i.e., failure respectively of one or two testicles to fully descend into the scrotum). In-breeding is never recommended and anyone who is not a very experienced breeder should avoid it.

- **Line-breeding.** This is a more 'distant' form of breeding than in-breeding and, if carefully and responsibly controlled, is the best way of ensuring the continuance of a successful line. The aim is to mate dogs with the same blood lines to achieve the desired results of temperament and conformation. Dogs of excellent quality are mated with related dogs of similar quality in order to improve upon and cement desired characteristics in the offspring. Father/granddaughter, mother/grandson, aunt/nephew, uncle/niece, half-brother/sister and cousin/cousin are all examples of selected line-breeding.

Great care must be taken to ensure both dog and bitch are sound and healthy, and they must possess an unmistakable likeness to each other. Only dogs and bitches of the highest quality, and free from any serious constructional faults, should be considered for this type of breeding. For sound and healthy offspring, line-breeding must not go too far, in particular avoiding mating between dogs that are very closely related on both sides of their respective pedigrees in recent generations. Carefully selected out-crosses to new quality blood lines must be included in any line-breeding programme. This enables the production of high-quality puppies free from any deterioration in health and conformation. Without this periodic input of fresh blood lines, line-breeding will eventually degenerate. It is all too easy for breeders to overlook this vital aspect of line-breeding.

- **Outcrossing.** This is the mating between an unrelated dog and bitch who do not possess a common ancestry. This type of breeding may be intended to introduce certain desirable characteristics into a litter of puppies. When successful, such breeding may produce occasional outstanding puppies – but remember that it is just as likely to result in faults inherited from either one or both parents. The drawback with this type of mating is that, because of the inconsistent fusion of unrelated genes, it becomes difficult to form a line that is clearly identifiable by type, uniformity and virtues.

This lack of uniformity can result in litters with puppies of different sizes and colours. It is something of a lottery, as desirable qualities – and faults – may not appear in first generation offspring, but only in the second generation. Such an outcrossing may be required to bring in new blood to a line. It also appears that outcrossing may well be advantageous to the health of the puppies because of the broad spread of genes.

CHOOSING A STUD DOG

It is important that you make the right choice. Do not cut corners and simply use the dog next door for the sake of convenience. Armed with a knowledge of the breeding alternatives described above, a prospective breeder will care-

Mother and daughter.

TRACKING DOWN A SUITABLE STUD DOG

A thorough study of the bitch's pedigree will reveal a pattern of breeding between certain dogs and bitches over the last four generations. (Anything beyond those four generations is irrelevant to this type of evaluation.) The purpose of the study is to identify those dogs and bitches whose positive and relatively fault-free attributes have been passed on to the bitch in question.

A study of the pedigrees of potential stud dogs may enable the identification of a particular dog with a significantly similar ancestry (though avoiding in-breeding). If that dog is sound in both health and conformation, then he may be selected to mate with the bitch, and the likelihood is that they will produce an even litter possessing the attributes and characteristics of the parents.

fully consider many factors before making a final decision in the selection of the right stud dog.

A male Staffordshire Bull Terrier's sexual potency will gradually decline after the age of seven years, and this should be taken into account. It does not mean an older dog cannot father puppies, but the chances of success are lower, unless he has been regularly sexually active and proven to sire healthy puppies. Success in the show ring is no guarantee that he will be the right dog for the bitch. He may be a top champion of the breed, but 'one-off' top-quality dogs can emerge from a litter of otherwise poor-quality puppies from less well bred parents. Thus a careful check of his pedigree is required to establish which dogs are influential in his blood lines, and to work out their compatibility with your bitch. There are of course great champions of the breed that are very dominant in their ability to influence the quality of the puppies they sire. Such dogs will have proven their valuable contribution to the breed by their considerable success in passing on their unmistakable qualities to the numerous puppies they have sired. But a pedigree loaded with champions of the breed does not necessarily imply the dog's prowess as a good stud dog.

Using a recognized stud dog, particularly if he is a popular champion, will have the benefit of helping you to sell the puppies, although there is no guarantee that they will have inherited his qualities. In fact, it could well be that an

A fully health tested and well bred stud dog: Champion Kyraloebis Italian Gigalo JwShCM, bred and owned by Rosaline Ann Plant.

Breeding, Pregnancy and Whelping

unheralded litter brother of a champion is as good if not better as a stud dog than his famous brother! The temperament of a prospective stud dog should never be anything less than perfect. Always remember the 'bold, fearless and totally reliable' comment in the Breed Standard, and never settle for less.

Never select a dog for stud that is too closely bred to the bitch as such a mating would be risky. No reasonable person would care to breed puppies with the likelihood of any of them possessing serious defects in health or conformation.

It is important to know whether the prospective stud dog is Kennel Club registered. Using an unregistered parent is likely to lead to disappointment, as any puppies, no matter how perfect, will never have pedigree status, and nor will any of their progeny. Unregistered Staffords cannot be shown at Kennel Club dog shows.

Agreements for a mating usually require the bitch to be taken to the dog. Remember to take into account the distance you will need to travel, and be sure to provide facilities for the comfort and welfare of the bitch on long journeys. It is most important for the owner of the bitch to let the owner of the dog know when the bitch is expected to come into season, and then notify them when it happens. This ensures that the mating can take place on the correct date.

Terms for a mating must be clearly agreed in advance. The stud fee must be agreed, along with any restrictions imposed by the stud dog owner on the showing or subsequent transfer of puppies should this become necessary. Conditions such as the pick of the litter in lieu of a stud fee must be made absolutely clear at the outset, as should the arrangements if the bitch fails to produce any puppies from the mating. In this case, it is usual for the stud dog owner to allow a free second mating during the bitch's next season, if desired. If possible, it is best to have a written agreement between the respective owners regarding all aspects of the breeding arrangement. Most owners of prominent stud dogs will have this already arranged.

Ensure that the chosen stud dog has been health tested for HC and L2HGA and has passed as clear. Alternatively, it may be shown on his Kennel Club documentation that he is hereditarily clear of both diseases. Most Kennel Club registered dogs and bitches are clear. A stud dog or a bitch that has or carries either of these problems will be declared to be a carrier, and will be capable of passing on the problem to any progeny. The puppies can be tested, and may be classed as either clear or unaffected, affected, or carriers. It is best always to ensure that both parents are completely clear, as this will give all the puppies hereditary clearness of the diseases.

Using a stud dog with a clear fault and the bitch possessing that same fault is asking for trouble and will only cement the problem in future generations. Often such a problem will then prove difficult to eliminate. Thus, the guide should be 'never put a fault to a fault'.

Should the bitch not be tall enough, putting her to a stud dog that is too tall will not solve the problem in the resulting puppies. Likewise, if a bitch is taller than the desirable height requirement, mating her with a dog that is too short will not produce puppies of the correct height. In both cases the litters will generally consist of some dogs that will become too tall and some that will become too short. The answer, as with any fault, is to mate the bitch to a standard size stud dog in an attempt to eliminate the problem. A larger proportion of the resulting litter should meet the height requirements of the Breed Standard.

If it will be your bitch's first litter, try to select an experienced stud dog. Such a dog will know exactly what he has to do, and the mating should be that much less stressful for the bitch.

It is worth having a plan for an alternative stud dog as a back-up should your primary choice become unavailable at the critical time. Otherwise, it may be best to wait for the bitch's next season to complete the original arrangements.

THE BITCH

A bitch will normally come into season – 'oestrous' or 'heat' – for the first time when she is about eight to nine months of age, although the timing can vary considerably. Thereafter the normal cycle for a bitch occurs about every six months.

No bitch should be considered for mating during her first season.

The heat normally lasts for twenty-one days and goes through the following stages:

- Initially the bitch has a heavy discharge of bright-coloured blood. This lasts for eight to nine days, and usually during this time she will show no interest in male dogs.
- Between the ninth and fifteenth days the discharge diminishes and becomes watery pink in colour. The vulva becomes larger and more swollen. During this critical seven-day period a bitch will be ready and willing to receive a dog, and this is the best time for her to be mated, ideally between the twelfth and fourteenth days.
- The season starts to finish on the fifteenth day and stops on the twenty-first. During this period the bitch's interest in male dogs will diminish and she may even become aggressive if approached by a dog.

PREPARING FOR THE MATING

You should know roughly when your bitch is about to commence her season, and you need to observe her closely so you don't miss the start of it. The timing is important, as this will enable the mating to take place at the optimum time. Her season can be said to start on the first day on which she begins to show 'colour'. The first sign is usually a plentiful discharge of brightly coloured blood, which can be anticipated by gently taking regular swabs of the vaginal area until the first sign of blood is clearly present. The swabbing process can be helpful as bitches tend to keep themselves clean and you may miss the start of the discharge.

In most cases, the optimum time for mating a bitch with a stud dog is during the twelfth to the fourteenth day after the commencement of her season. This is the time of her maximum ovulation, and a successful mating at this time should produce a full litter of puppies. This is not always the case, but it is a good yardstick.

As soon as you have a definite date, contact the owner of the stud dog to finalize the arrangements. If there is any uncertainty about the start date, a second mating a few days after the first may well overcome any miscalculation. Remember also that the dog's sperm can be effectively retained for several days after a mating and can successfully fertilize ova released later. There will, however, be a gradual decline in the chances of successful reproduction.

The bitch determines the number of puppies in a litter according to the number of ova she produces.

Although rare, some bitches display variations from the normal season. A 'silent' heat occurs when a bitch shows no sign of the normal coloured discharge, although she is in full heat. It is difficult in such circumstances to judge accurately the optimum time for a mating. The bitch may show that she is ready to be mated if she 'stands' as if ready to accept a dog, curling her tail round to her side when stimulated by a hand stroking the fur around the base of her tail. At such a time the introduction of a dog may certainly have the desired results of a successful mating and subsequent pregnancy. Silent heats may be due to a hormone deficiency. Veterinary advice should be sought regarding hormonal injections in order to rectify the problem for subsequent heats.

Another unusual problem with some bitches is the 'false' heat. In such cases a bitch will show every indication that she is coming into full heat. Her vaginal area will swell up and a discharge of brightly coloured blood will begin. This will not last, however, and she will quickly revert back to normal. During that phase, however, she may well stand for a dog and show all the signs of a natural season. A dog may actually mate with her but conception will not take place. After the bitch has herself returned to normal, a full complete season may quickly follow.

When to mate your bitch

As discussed earlier, the most successful time for your bitch to be mated is at the precise time of maximum ovulation, and guidance has been given on how best to obtain a valid estimate of that time. What, then, if your bitch, despite the most careful preparations, does not produce any puppies? This is disappointing, but she will come back into season in another six months and you can try again. In the meantime, you can consider what may have gone wrong. The bitch may be carrying an infection, which will require veterinary attention. There is, of course, a possibility that it was the fault of the stud dog, but this is unlikely with a proven stud dog. Owners of stud dogs are only too aware that it is the opinion of some owners of bitches that it is the dog who is always at fault. However, it is far more likely that an error was made in the timing of the mating.

The problem may be due to over-reliance on the recommended twelve to fourteen day window. If a bitch has missed – and certainly if she continues to miss – then it may be that the timing of her ovulation differs from the norm. In the case of such a bitch, no definite time can be given for her mating. There have been instances of some bitches standing for a dog ready for mating well before the tenth day and even many days after the twenty-first day of her season. Sadly, such bitches are often mistakenly considered barren. In fact, if mated at their individual peak of ovulation they will produce lovely litters of puppies. Similarly, some bitches have just a very short period in their window of ovulation, sometimes as short as just a few hours. Just how with any certainty can a satisfactory mating be accurately performed in such cases?

Don't despair! There are ways. For example, good results are claimed from examining the microscopic patterns of swabs from the bitch's vagina for the changes that indicate when she is ovulating. Special probes are available for insertion into the vagina, which will also indicate the correct time for mating. Blood tests can also determine the optimum time of ovulation. Personal experience has shown that the results from such blood tests are not always satisfactory and the bitch concerned has proved to be not ready for mating at the time indicated.

There are companies that specialize in this type of testing. Upon application, you will be supplied with all that is required to carry out the tests, including collection tubes for blood samples. A veterinary surgeon will take a small quantity of blood from the bitch, and this is despatched for next day delivery to be tested. The results of the test will be telephoned on the same day directly to the breeder, saying that either further tests are necessary or the bitch is ready for mating. At some point you will be told that the optimum ovulation time is present and you should mate the bitch immediately. These tests can take place at any time from the commencement of the bitch's season and can extend beyond the normal twenty-one days if necessary. The advantage of this procedure is that even the most irregular season can be accommodated. It is relatively expensive, but the results can make it well worth considering.

Another way to get the timing for a mating right is to introduce a healthy male dog. He must not, of course, be allowed to run free with the bitch but needs to be close to her. His natural instincts will let you know when the magic hour arrives. You may have to put up with a few nights of groaning and howling in frustration, but when the noise reaches crescendo proportions that is when to take your bitch to the stud dog. This procedure often works well, but do bear in mind that some bitches are sexually attractive to a male dog throughout the whole season, not necessarily just at the point of ovulation.

THE MATING

Look out for the presence of a slight milky discharge, accompanied by a swelling of the vulva. At this time the bitch will probably be paying more attention than usual to cleaning herself up. This is the time to take her to the stud dog. Make sure that all is in place regarding pedigree and health certificates.

Do not feed the bitch for twelve hours or so before mating. Do in particular make sure the bitch is equipped with a large, substantial collar. There must be enough room for a firm grip to be taken of both sides of the collar and still allow the bitch to breathe properly.

The general procedure is to take your bitch to the stud dog. This can sometimes involve a considerable journey. Your bitch, particularly if

Breeding, Pregnancy and Whelping

A bitch showing she is ready, presenting herself to the dog/stud.

this is her first time, may well suffer some anxiety and stress in unfamiliar surroundings, so it can help if members of her family are there to comfort her and give her confidence. She will settle down much more quickly if she has her owners with her. Always insist there is at least one person present who has experience of the procedures involved in the mating of dogs.

Should the bitch become difficult, resist any attempt to have her muzzled. This is cruel. Most bitches will be ready to accept a dog if the timing is right. If it is not, they can be very difficult to handle. It may be best to wait a day and try again. An inexperienced dog can also unsettle a bitch, causing her to behave aggressively or entirely refuse to co-operate. This is where someone experienced in mating of dogs is required to help. As long as the stud dog is experienced, all will probably go well even when mating with an inexperienced maiden bitch.

Some stud dog owners believe that natural mating is the best way and will want the dogs to manage the mating on their own and without interference. My advice is that you insist the mating be controlled. You are dealing with two powerful Staffordshire Bull Terriers who don't know each other, and things could turn extremely nasty if the bitch does not accept the dog's advances.

Sit on a chair in front of the bitch and hold her collar on both sides so that she cannot turn her head and snap at the dog as he attempts to mate her. The dog can then be allowed to follow his natural instincts to mount her. Particularly with a young inexperienced bitch, she may become alarmed when the dog attempts to penetrate her, which may cause her to thrash about, This can cause injury to the dog. To prevent this happening, she should be soothed and encouraged. If the dog experiences difficulties in achiev-

Breeding, Pregnancy and Whelping

DIFFICULTIES WITH MATING

Occasionally it happens that a bitch takes an instant dislike to the dog chosen for her, and becomes frighteningly aggressive towards him. Others may resist any attempt by the dog to mate with her. Our family has over forty years' experience in breeding Staffords, and over that time we developed a method that makes the whole event go as smoothly as possible, even with nervous bitches.

The owners may have travelled a long way to bring their bitch for this important mating and the first thing is to make them welcome in a relaxed and friendly manner. The stud dog will not be present when the bitch is brought in, and she should be allowed free rein to find her way around. When she is relaxed, she can be checked to make sure she's ready, and then the owner will be asked to take her outside, on her lead, to the entrance to the premises. The stud dog, also on a lead, will be gently introduced to her there. When he gets her scent he will know what to do, and her response to him will be noted. She may show great interest, or she may growl and warn him to keep his distance. Either way, allow them time to become accustomed to each other. Go for a gentle five minute walk together, with the dogs side by side. The stud dog will certainly be showing her a lot of attention, and will try to move round to sniff her. Again she may succumb to this quite happily or she may show resentment. Gradually allow him to get closer. All this takes only a few minutes and even an aggressive bitch will gradually calm down as she realizes that the stud dog is not a threat. This approach has worked admirably for many years.

When the dogs are ready, take them back to the house for a controlled hands-on mating. A non-slip mat should be ready, with a chair at one end for the handler. The bitch is placed on the mat, and the handler sits on the chair and takes hold of her collar. Only then is the dog brought in and the mating can proceed in a calm, controlled way. This method generally helps to keep even a nervous bitch calm, so that the experience is not unpleasant for her.

Not every stud dog owner follows this method, but it works well for an inexperienced bitch and is worth discussing.

After a satisfactory mating.

Breeding, Pregnancy and Whelping

ing penetration, an experienced person will be needed to guide the dog's penis into the bitch's vulva. After penetration, he should be held firmly there for a short while until a tie is achieved. Should a tie not happen, the dog should be held in place for some time longer. The tie will confirm that seminal fluid has been ejaculated into the bitch.

The tie

The tie occurs at the conclusion of a successful coupling when the dog turns around so that the pair are tail to tail while his penis is still inside her vulva. For the most reasonable explanation for this phenomenon, one has to turn to nature. In the wild it may have enabled the mating pair to defend themselves while still linked together, and prevented any other mating taking place immediately.

When the dog ejaculates, he pumps millions of sperm into the bitch. At this stage his penis will have swollen up to three or four times its normal size and changed its shape. The resulting 'golf-ball' shape half way up the penis holds the two dogs firmly together until deflation takes place and allows for the release.

It is always reassuring when a ties takes place, but it is not always necessary. A 'slip' mating can achieve the same result, but without the tie taking place. Our family had the privilege of owning the top stud dog in the breed for many years, and that prolific and highly successful dog tied only twice during his lifetime.

During the tie the bitch will usually relax and the dog will start to fidget and want to turn. He may need help to lift one of his hind legs over the bitch's back so he can turn around. The end result is that the dog and bitch end up tail to tail facing opposite directions. They will normally be quite comfortable. They should be gently held in that position by their collars to prevent any damage if one of them tries to pull away from the other. The tie can last from a few minutes up to an hour, and sometimes even longer, but usually it can be expected to last for between fifteen minutes and half an hour. After the dog is released from the tie, he should be removed from the scene and given a drink of water and allowed to rest. The bitch should be made a great fuss of, given water to drink and where possible allowed to run around. She will normally be quite happy, wagging her tail and showing she is pleased with herself.

Thirty-one days pregnant and her 'tuck up' is beginning to disappear.

PREGNANCY

The normal gestation period is sixty-three days, although this can vary, especially if the bitch was mated more than once. For the first few days there will be no evidence of pregnancy but from the outset you must concentrate all your attention on ensuring your bitch's welfare. Assuming you are already feeding her a satisfactory and beneficial diet, then don't change it, and don't increase her intake of food in the mistaken belief that this will be of benefit to the puppies. It won't – it will just make her fat. Worse, it may make the puppies fat, and this may cause trouble for your bitch during the birthing process. During the final weeks you can change to one of the special diets formulated to support lactating bitches. These are designed to be fed to the mother up to completion of the weaning stage, and from then onwards can be given to the puppies as their first solid food.

Your bitch should be given her regular exercise right up to the time of whelping as long as she is comfortable and keen to go for walks. Obviously great care must be taken with a heavily pregnant bitch, and it is advisable not to go too far from home. If she shows signs of discomfort let her rest.

An observant owner may notice subtle change in the bitch's behaviour and personality as she prepares for motherhood. Even in the early stages of pregnancy, for example, she may avoid the rough play of other dogs. These are encouraging signs but are not necessarily in themselves evidence of pregnancy. In the first four weeks or so there will be little evidence of the developing puppies, and you may begin to wonder whether your bitch actually is pregnant. Your veterinary surgeon may be able to determine the presence of puppies by feeling her abdomen, or there is a blood test that can be done, but the surest way is via an ultrasound scan at around twenty-eight days after mating. The scanning process is simple and absolutely painless, and will confirm whether your bitch is pregnant, and roughly how many puppies she is carrying. (It isn't 100 per cent accurate as the puppies are very small at this stage, and one or two may be hidden from the scanner.)

Scanning does not always produce good news. On one occasion one of my bitches was shown to have a deadly enclosed pyometra (a uterine infection). I took her straight to the vet and insisted that he carry out an emergency operation. A massive pyometra was removed. This almost certainly saved the bitch's life.

Some owners like to have another scan done towards the end of pregnancy. By this stage the puppies will be fully visible, and an assessment can be made of their presentation. This can be of considerable benefit as it will give a very good idea of what can be expected during whelping.

PREPARING FOR WHELPING

You will need a whelping box, with arrangements for heating, and some form of emergency container for transporting the newly born puppies to the vet should the need arise. The whelping box must be substantially built as it will be the home of both the bitch and her puppies for several weeks after the birth. Certainly it must be large enough to comfortably contain the mother and her new young family and should be designed for ease of access. A box that is not too deep will be helpful for cleaning. There are various excellent whelping boxes that can be purchased commercially – just make certain you buy one of the right size for your Stafford – or, for a handyman, it is not so difficult to design and build one at home. The access point needs a partition to contain the puppies, while allowing the bitch to jump in and out. A 'pig rail' will be required around the walls. This strip of wood, approximately 8 cm wide and set about the same measurement above the base, enables puppies to crawl to safety should the mother accidentally lie on them. The environment of the newly born puppies must be kept at a fairly high temperature, starting at about 25 °Celsius (75 °Fahrenheit) and gradually decreasing during the first few weeks. A temperature-controlled heat lamp securely suspended at a safe height above the whelping box is ideal for the purpose; such lamps are widely available.

The emergency container can consist of a cardboard box or even a washing-up bowl. It should

Breeding, Pregnancy and Whelping

The opinions of an expert sonographer are valuable to anyone interested in understanding the procedures and complexities of scanning. Barbara Wiseman (Wisescan), the distinguished pioneer and researcher into the practice of scanning dogs, was approached and asked if she would write a short contribution. She kindly agreed, and with her permission her response is given below. It contains much very sound advice and deserves to be read by anyone wishing to breed a litter of Staffordshire Bull Terriers.

SCANNING BY BARBARA WISEMAN (WISESCAN)

This should be carried out at around 28 days from the first mating to achieve maximum accuracy on numbers and prediction of whelping date (see the following for an explanation of possible whelping anomalies).

Because ova take a few days to mature, the duration of the pregnancy can vary from between 56 days to 66 days in terms of the timing of ovulation and also, as the sperm can remain viable within the vagina for some time, this period can be extended to up to 70 days from mating.

The further on in the pregnancy the bitch is, the harder it is to count numbers as one foetus may obscure another, and therefore counting is more accurate in the early stages. Unfortunately not all the foeti may be visible and some may be lost during the pregnancy so that the scanning can only give an estimate of numbers. This, however, is better than having no idea at all, as the diet can be restricted in the case of small litters. If upon scanning no pregnancy is seen, the pregnancy may not yet be of 28th day duration and it will be necessary to repeat the scan a few days later.

Early scanning will also pick up potential pyometra risk (your sonographer [scanner] must be competent to identify this accurately as it can very quickly become life-threatening if left untreated). **Early pregnancy and pyometra can resemble each other to the untrained eye.**

If you miss this scanning window (between 28 and 35 days) entirely, it is difficult to get information from the scan beyond the fact that the bitch is pregnant. However, as this is the only certain determination of pregnancy, the information will still have some use.

Having scanned early and having a projected date of whelping and an estimate of numbers, a second scan should be completed at 56 days. This should give a good idea of the ease of whelping as both foetal size and presentation are evident.

Having studied bitch pregnancies over 30 years there are a few thoughts I would like to share:
Although there are several aids on the market to assist with the determination of ovulation, it seems to me too much dependence is being placed on these aids as I am now seeing a far higher rate of failure and I believe this is because we are forgetting to look at all the signs that the bitch is ready and willing to be mated. Any test can only suggest the probability of the onset of oestrus when the bitch should be mated.

The luteinizing hormone peak which occurs during the 'season' is regarded as being the central event of the bitch's cycle and events after this peak take place as follows:

Ovulation	48 hours
Oocyte (eggs) maturation	4–5 days (2–3 days post ovulation)
Implantation	18 days
Parturition (whelping)	64–66 days

It is generally accepted that sperm can remain viable for up to seven days (I myself have scanned a bitch who showed no signs of pregnancy until 38 days after a single mating and went on to produce six healthy puppies on day 72 post mating). It is therefore not possible to be certain that there is no pregnancy until 35 days post mating.

Although most bitches ovulate between 10 and 14 days from the start of their season, this requires the owner to know when the season started. Most of the signs we look for are a human interpretation of the start of the season and therefore can be seriously inaccurate. It seems that allowing your bitch to have access to a male (without allowing mating, of course) can be a most accurate way of determining when a bitch is ready.

Assuming your bitch is successfully pregnant, there are major changes to be taken into account: firstly the immune system is compromised to allow the introduction of the sperm and the growth of the foetus without the body rejecting same. Care should be taken regarding exposure to possible infective sites outside the bitch's usual environment in the first two weeks.

Secondly the bitch's metabolic rate alters, enabling her to better utilize her food. The same is true in humans, hence the advice to every pregnant woman that she should not eat for two. Over the past 30 years I have tried very hard to dissuade overfeeding of pregnant bitches but I am currently seeing a return to an unnecessary increase in the number of caesarean deliveries. Exercise is also very important during pregnancy, as being fit and lean enables the bitch in an uncomplicated pregnancy to whelp with ease.

MY CREDENTIALS

The Roslin Institute in Penicuik, Scotland, forms part of the research unit of the Scottish Agricultural College. A project was developed at the Institute in 1982/3 to ascertain whether it was possible to use ultrasonic scanning to determine foetal numbers in sheep to avoid metabolic disorders common to sheep carrying multiple lambs.

I attended a training course at Roslin in 1983 and in 1984 started scanning sheep. I already had an interest in working dogs and wondered whether the technique would be of use in pregnancy in bitches. At the time looking at a pregnancy was only possible during operations to open up the bitch, and therefore there were many myths surrounding pregnancy. For two years I invited anyone with a pregnant bitch to let me scan her to see what information could be derived. I charted every scan and recorded every outcome and built up my knowledge year after year. Despite this, 30 years later, I still see things I have never seen before, making me realize how complex life actually is.

In terms of ovulation, I had advertised in the dog papers that I had an infallible method of determining pregnancy (i.e. scanning) and was approached by Dr D. Anderson of the company, who subsequently went on to develop Premate as they were trying to develop a blood test to determine pregnancy. This had proved unsatisfactory and I was invited up to Cambridge to discuss it. My charts mentioned above showed anomalies in the apparent growth of the pregnancy and it soon became apparent that this and their blood test failure rate were down to not knowing when ovulation took place.

Premate was about to be launched and I brought home a few of the original kits, which were actually pig tests, and dispensed them to local vets who had shown an interest in my scanning. We had 100 per cent success in getting bitches pregnant using it, mainly on previous failures, and from that, my interest in all aspects of canine pregnancy have grown.

Breeding, Pregnancy and Whelping

A whelping pen.

be of a sensible size and comfortably lined so the newborn puppies can be kept warm. A hot water bottle well wrapped up in a towel is useful.

Place the whelping box in an easily accessible place in the home. There should be ample light, and it must be warm. A heat lamp set above the whelping box is the ideal solution. Put the whelping box in place well before the puppies are due and encourage the bitch into it by feeding her in it. You can put her bed in there and try to get her to sleep in the box. This way it will become hers and she will happily have her puppies in it.

As the whelping date approaches, you will need to prepare the box by adding bedding material. This must be something that the young puppies cannot squirm beneath or suffocate under. A good supply of newspapers is also a good idea. Lay them in the whelping box and let your bitch tear them up in response to her instinctive need to dig out a den for her puppies. Notify your vet of the expected date of birth so that help is available in an emergency. Keep the vet's contact numbers available, and make sure you have transport available should you need to get to the vet quickly.

It is useful to have a small bottle of brandy to hand – a few drops mixed into some milk can be a useful stimulant. Just to be on the safe side, a milk substitute (available from your vet) and a baby's bottle to feed it with will be essential if your bitch fails to produce enough milk initially.

A ready supply of cleaning materials and rough towels must be on hand at the time of birth, and surgical gloves, a reliable thermometer and sharp scissors may be useful.

There will be times when the mother will need to get away from the vigorous attentions of her puppies for a little peace and quiet. Place a comfortable bed for her beside the whelping box.

WHELPING

About six weeks into her pregnancy the bitch's abdomen will start to increase in size and her mammary glands and teats will start to enlarge. Her appetite will most likely remain good, but remember not to overfeed her at this stage in the false belief it will be of advantage to the unborn puppies. About a week before she is due to give birth, milk may start to ooze from her teats.

There is no reason to expect whelping difficulties for Staffordshire Bull Terriers. Staffords are physically strong dogs, but they still need reassurance and support at this time, even when things are progressing normally. Should things go wrong, you will need to contact with your veterinary surgeon immediately. If you are concerned, do not hesitate - it could be fatal, either to the bitch or to her puppies.

Normally, a gestation period of around 63 days is to be expected, but it is not uncommon, especially with a first-timer, for a bitch to produce her litter up to five days early. This is nothing to worry about. The puppies may appear at first to be a little backward and immature but they will very quickly catch up. With such puppies, it may

Breeding, Pregnancy and Whelping

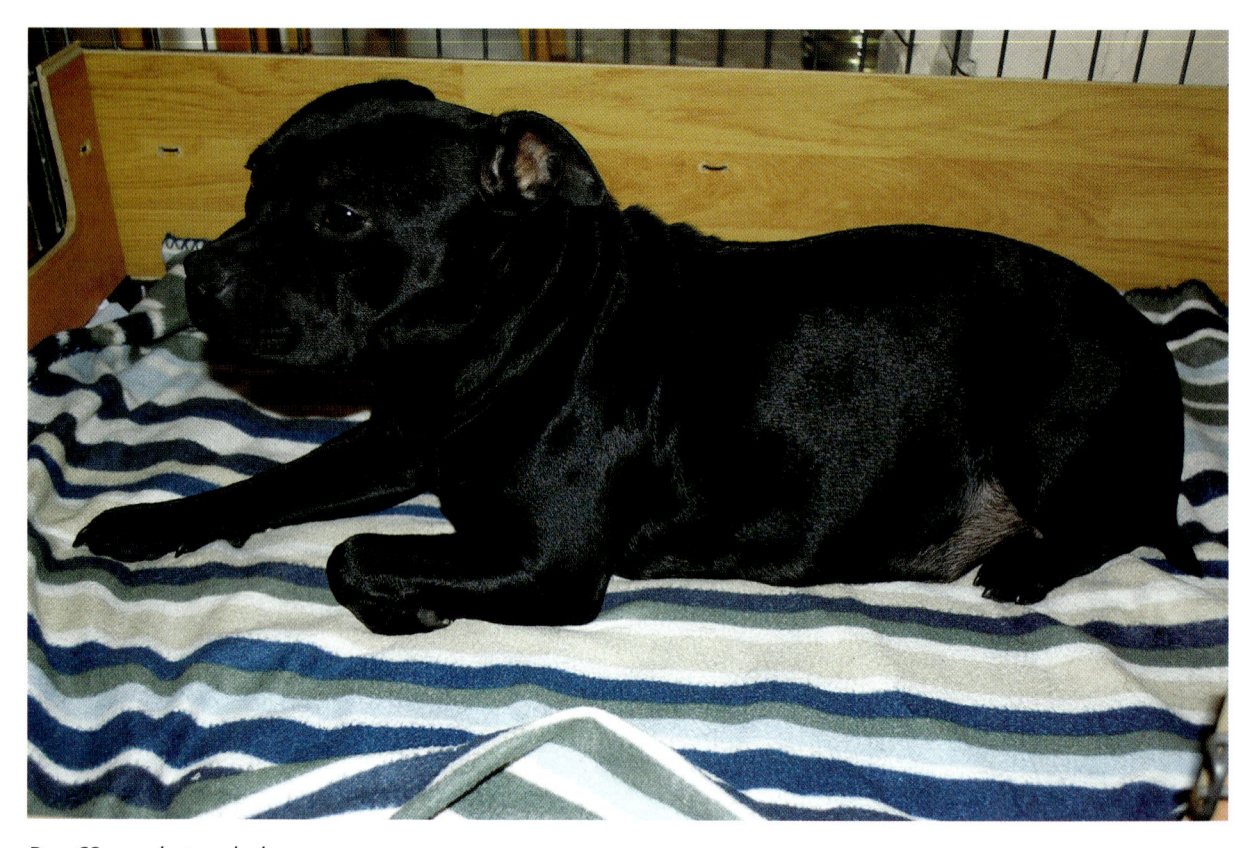

Day 63: ready to whelp.

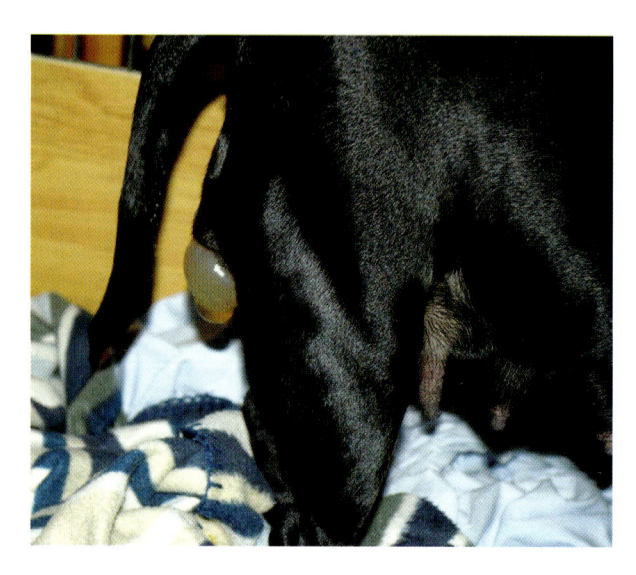

The first puppy is arriving: the water bag appears first.

take a little more time for their eyes to open than the normal ten or so days.

A drop in the bitch's temperature to below 100° Fahrenheit is likely to herald labour. It is not always the case, but usually she will not want any food or drink and will become agitated in her attempts to dig out a nest (preferably in her whelping box) by tearing up any bedding or newspapers laid down for the purpose. After this period of scratching and fidgeting, she may sleep for a while – this seems to be Nature's way of preparing her for the ordeal ahead.

A slight rippling of the muscles along her back will indicate that the bitch is about to go into labour. After a while the straining and rippling of her contractions will become more regular until they can be observed several times a minute. At about this time a fluid-filled 'balloon' about the size of a golf ball will appear outside the

Breeding, Pregnancy and Whelping

bitch's vulva. The purpose of this water bag is to act as a cushion to protect the emerging puppy against pressure. When the water bag ruptures and releases its contents, the puppy should follow within a few minutes. If this does not happen, and the puppy still hasn't arrived within an hour, contact your vet. You may need to take the bitch to the surgery. There is no need for undue

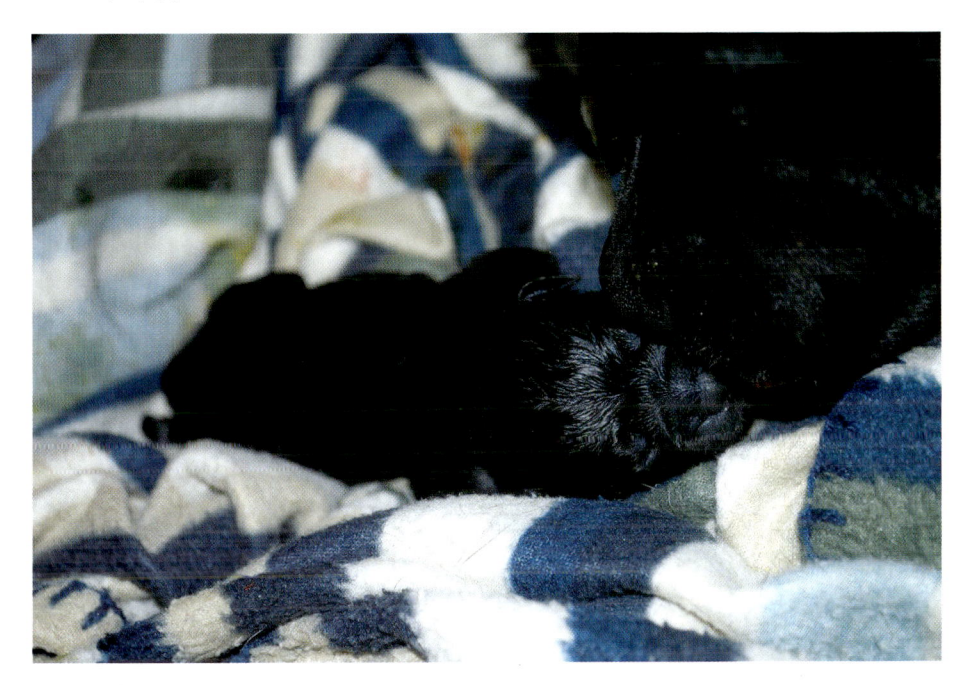

The first puppy is born and the mother is very attentive, cleaning her newborn.

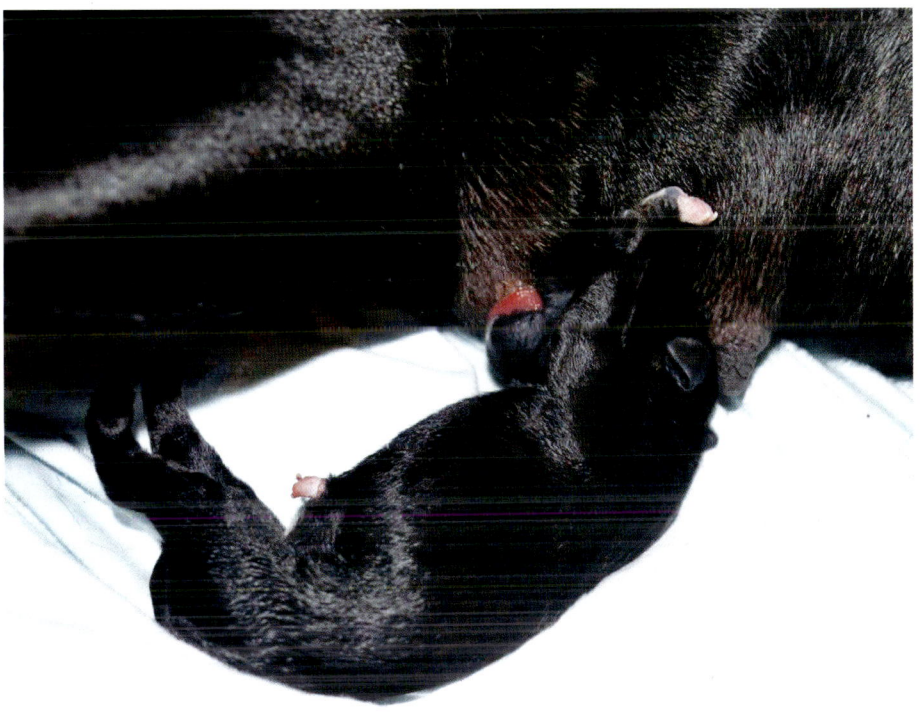

The newborn puppy suckling.

Breeding, Pregnancy and Whelping

concern should this happen. The puppy will no doubt eventually arrive, and sometimes with the motion of the car it will arrive during the journey! This has happened to the author more than once.

Puppies normally arrive head first. Some arrive feet first, which is a nuisance but should not cause complications, especially in a Staffordshire Bull Terrier. Each puppy is born inside an amniotic sac, which normally ruptures during birth. If it doesn't, it must be torn open to allow the puppy to breathe. An experienced bitch will immediately turn and get the puppy out of the sac by licking and biting at it. Her instinct tells her to clean the puppy and her vigorous licking stimulates the puppy to breathe.

An inexperienced bitch may be bewildered by the whole birth process and not know what to do with this first puppy. If this happens, tear the bag and use a towel to gently clear any mucus away from the puppy's mouth so it can fill its lungs and start breathing. Then, wrap a rough towel around the puppy and massage his chest firmly and rhythmically. This promotes the commencement of normal respiration by the initial intake of breath. If the puppy does not respond to this, you must act quickly. You may need to give the 'kiss of life' by breathing gently into his mouth.

At this stage the newborn puppy will still be attached by the umbilical cord to the placenta, which will still be inside the mother. If she does not expel the placenta naturally, the owner should help by gently taking hold of the umbilical cord between finger and thumb and carefully pulling it free. Some bitches will eat the placenta. This is normal. In the wild, a bitch will instinctively eat the placenta as this provides nourish-

'I have my new babies, now I can rest.'

ment at a time when she is temporarily incapacitated. The umbilical cord must never be pulled away from the puppy's tummy as this can cause an umbilical hernia, which may require corrective surgery later. Normally the bitch will instinctively turn, nip and sever the umbilical cord herself. If she doesn't, take hold of the cord well above the puppy's navel and, using strong cotton or surgical thread, tie it off in two places an inch or so apart. The cord can then be cut between the ties, using sterilized scissors. The mother will then nudge her newborn towards her teats, where the puppy will instinctively start to suckle.

After the first puppy, even the most inexperienced bitch will be able to whelp the remaining puppies. Between deliveries she may have a short sleep, Normally a puppy will be born within about twenty minutes or so of the onset of regular contractions, but sometimes it can take much longer. The time between puppies can vary between about ten minutes and an hour. If at any the bitch becomes exhausted, and her straining noticeably weaker, contact your veterinary surgeon urgently. It may be due to a condition known as uterine inertia, resulting in a puppy not being delivered. A caesarean operation will be necessary to save that puppy, and any other puppies following behind him.

If all goes well, then at the end of it you will be privileged to witness the wonderful sight of a relaxed and sleeping mother with a lovely litter of healthy newly born puppies murmuring and contentedly suckling away.

AFTER WHELPING

Once she has safely delivered all her puppies, the bitch will probably become calm and spend a lot of time cleaning and washing herself. She will need to go outside to perform her natural toilet functions but will be keen to get back to her puppies. Whilst she is out, change the bedding in the whelping box and clean up the whole area. Quickly examine each puppy to make sure they are healthy and there are no obvious abnormalities. As you clear up, if you have not already done so, check that there is an expelled placenta for each puppy. If not, a visit to the vet for an injection will be required in order to prevent any infection resulting from a retained placenta.

When she comes back to the puppies, offer the bitch a warm drink of half milk and half water. Some people add a dessertspoonful of honey. She should then be left in peace with her puppies. Strangers and noisy children should be kept well away, and the whelping box must be strictly off limits for all family pets. When agitated and confused by unwanted disruptions, bitches have been known to pick up their puppies and try to hide them away somewhere. This sometimes happens anyway, with some bitches inexplicably showing signs of restless nervousness and wanting to hide their puppies away. Calm and sympathetic attention and reassurance will be required from their owners.

A bitch who has just produced a litter of puppies will be exhausted from her ordeal and needs peace and quiet for a day or so. Immediately after recovering from the whelping her diet should consist of light meals such as scrambled eggs and filleted white fish. Offer her as much of the warm milk and water mixture as she wants. Bitches often suffer from diarrhoea after whelping, and it may be necessary to cut down on anything in her food that is likely to exacerbate this problem. You might consider changing her diet to one of the good quality complete diets formulated for lactating bitches. Certainly she will need a very nutritious diet to help her cope with the demands of her new puppies.

The bitch should be able to provide ample milk for her puppies, but sometimes this proves inadequate, especially in the first few days after birth. The puppies will not thrive and will be constantly crying. If this happens, it is essential to supplement the feeding until a regular milk supply is produced by the bitch. Use a baby feeding bottle and special synthetic milk available from your vet.

Satisfying the demands of a litter of growing puppies can result in the mother's blood calcium level falling too low. This results in a condition called eclampsia, and it can be fatal to the bitch. If affected, she will begin to show symptoms of nervousness and unsteadiness. This will rapidly progress to staggering and convulsions. An

Breeding, Pregnancy and Whelping

Feeding from mum.

We love porridge!

immediate injection of calcium by a vet is essential in order to save her life. This condition is most likely to set in when the puppies are about three weeks old. It is important to start weaning a large litter on to their first solid foods as soon as reasonably possible in order to give the mother some relief from their demands.

Over-suckling can lead to a condition known as mastitis. The teats and mammary glands will become very hard, hot and sore. The bitch should be checked regularly for symptoms, and taken straight to the vet if necessary for treatment.

The puppies can start to be weaned at about three weeks of age. A big bowl of warm porridge mixed with honey is a good way to start. Plop each puppy down into the food and sit back and enjoy their reaction! They will be covered in the food, and gradually they will start to lick at it. Most quickly catch on and get stuck in! When they have had enough, don't

Breeding, Pregnancy and Whelping

From porridge to puppy food.

worry about cleaning them up. The bitch will happily help out here. By about four weeks of age the puppies should be having several small meals a day, including a variety of meat and cereal foods, as well as milk.

Once their eyes are open and they are truly up on their feet, the puppies will start to clamber out of the whelping box. This is when you should begin the socializing process. By the time the puppies are twenty-eight days old they should all have been properly wormed and their nails trimmed. They should have been gently handled by all members of the family and given lots of opportunities to run around and play with plenty of challenging toys.

By the time the puppies are eight weeks old, they will have been weaned from their mother and will be ready to move on to their new homes. Your bitch will once again be fit and well, having done all she can to give her puppies a good, healthy start.

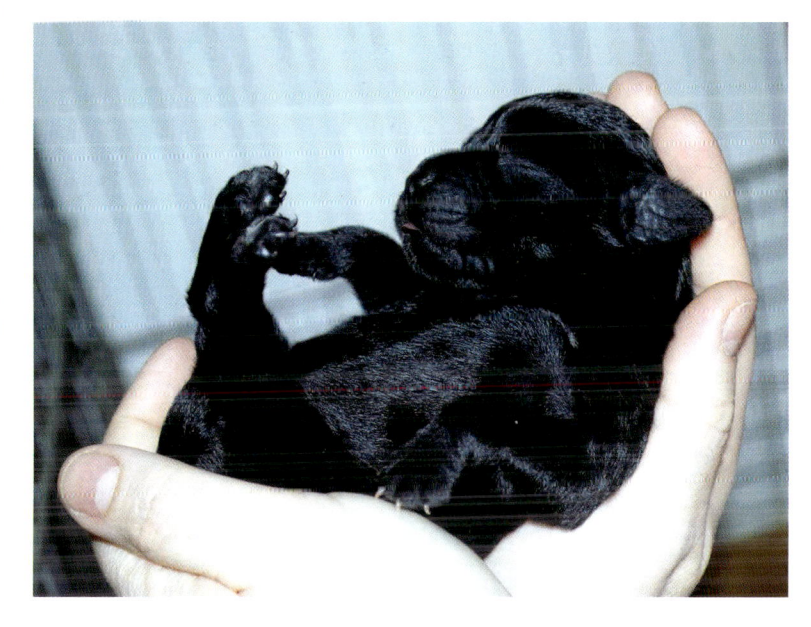

A newborn puppy, just a few hours old.

Breeding, Pregnancy and Whelping

Eight weeks old and ready for their new families.

9 ACCIDENTS, AILMENTS AND DISEASES

The Staffordshire Bull Terrier is a very healthy dog. Properly fed, well exercised and carefully looked after, he can be expected to live a long and active life, largely free from ailments and diseases. Nevertheless, accidents do happen, and there may be times when your Stafford falls ill. Knowing how best to react is of great importance to any owner. It is not always necessary to seek expert assistance: in the case of minor

FIRST AID KIT

An easily accessible first aid kit is an important item to have at home. It should contain the following items:

Bandages
Adhesive tape
Antiseptic liquid or cream
Milk of magnesia
Cotton wool
Ready cut gauze
Antibiotic skin ointment
Cotton-tipped swabs
Alcohol wipes
Rectal thermometer
Tweezers
Scissors
TCP solution
Iodine solution

First aid kits can be purchased from commercial pet suppliers. An additional kit kept in the family car is also worth considering.

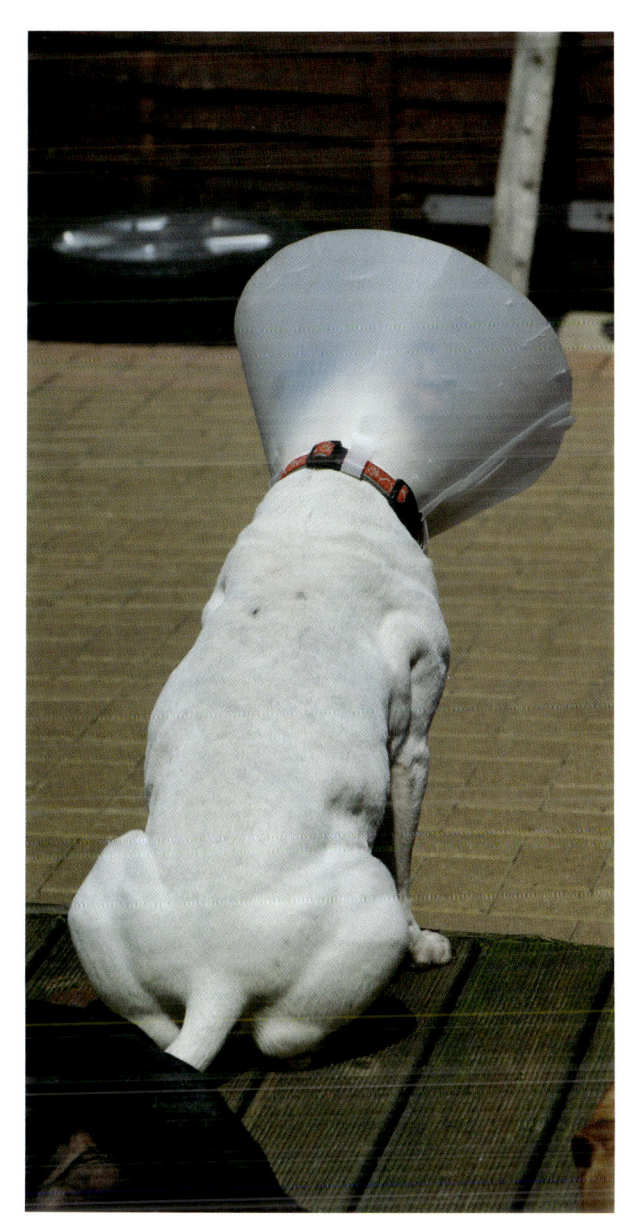

'I've just got to put up with this until I'm better!'

Accidents, Ailments and Diseases

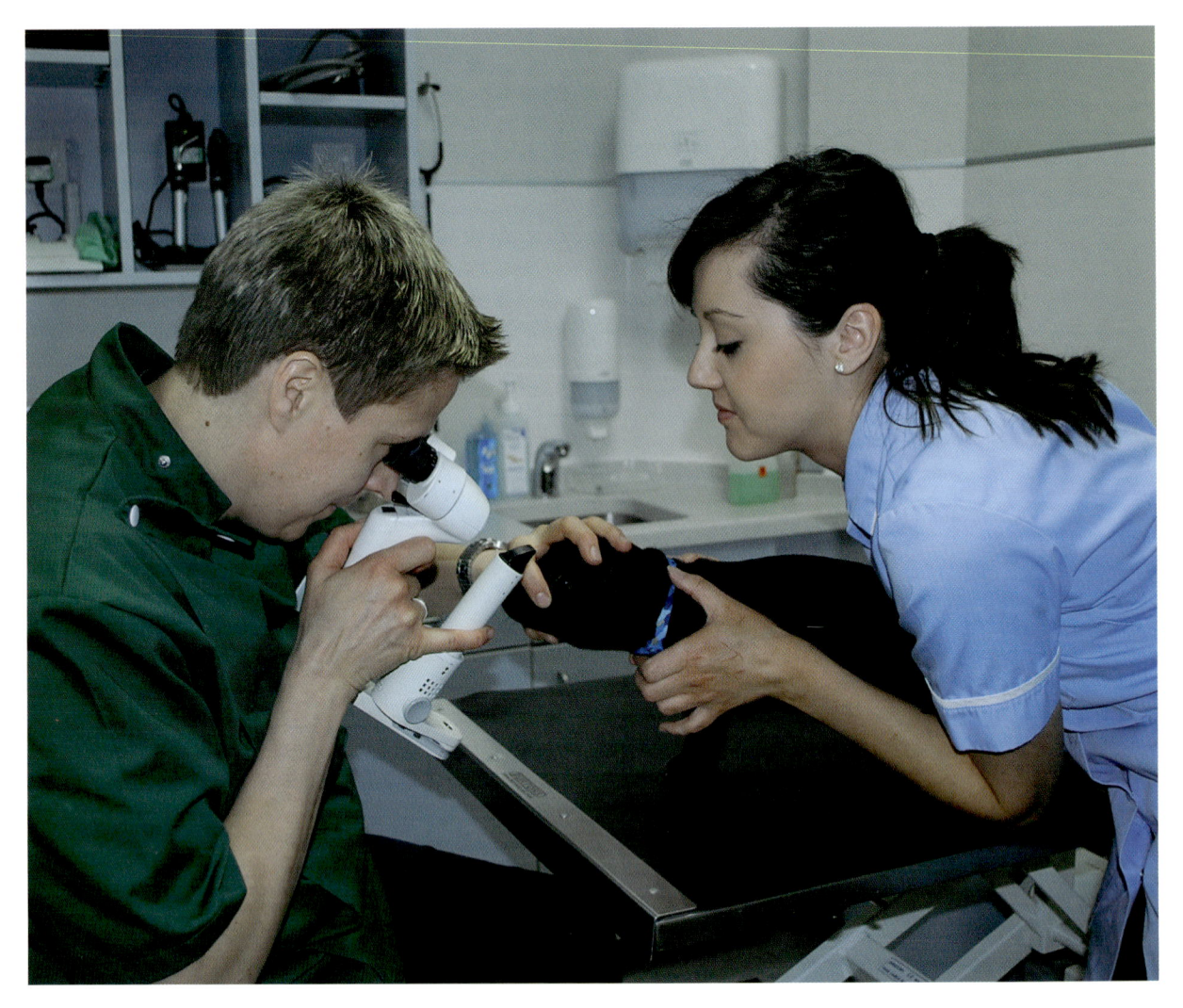

Eye screening a puppy for PHPV/PPSC as per current guidelines.

illnesses and injuries your dog can be looked after at home simply by applying common-sense care. For this purpose you should have in your home a canine first aid kit. For anything more serious, go to your vet. A good vet can be an owner's best friend in an emergency. It helps if you choose a surgery that has experience in treating Staffords, with their particularly high degree of pain tolerance. Always make sure the surgery's telephone number is at hand, but don't call out of normal practice hours unless it is an emergency.

ACCIDENTS

When an accident happens, the aims of first responders must be to prevent unnecessary suffering, to prevent further injury and perhaps even simply to keep the victim alive. Try to keep calm. Panicking or rushing into inappropriate action will not help the situation at all. Contact a vet, and explain the problem as clearly as possible. They will tell you what to do and despatch professional help. It helps to know how to move or lift a badly injured dog.

Accidents, Ailments and Diseases

A car accident didn't stop this dog having a long and happy life!

All of the following situations can be life-threatening and should be classed as an emergency:

- Shock
- Choking
- Not breathing
- Excessive loss of blood
- Severe burning or scalding
- Electrocution
- Collapse

DISEASES AND AILMENTS

Abscess An abscess can occur on any part of the dog's body. It shows as a shiny swelling under the skin, and is full of pus. In serious cases the dog's temperature may be raised. Veterinary attention should be sought.

Acne Skin inflammation that shows up in an eruption of pimples usually on the bridge of the nose or on the under-belly. The pimples will eventually burst, discharging a sticky pus, and

Accidents, Ailments and Diseases

turn into scabs. The dog will constantly scratch at the area; it is not necessarily painful, but will be irritating. Veterinary attention should be sought

Anaemia If you suspect anaemia, contact your vet as soon as possible. The correct pigmentation of the nose, lips and tongue will be absent, and the dog's appetite may deteriorate, with a noticeable loss of condition. He may also lose his enthusiasm for exercise or play. Your vet will take a blood sample for analysis, which will indicate the correct remedy.

Anal disorders Blocked anal glands will need to be squeezed out by a vet. Without proper attention, blocked glands can lead to painful anal abscesses. A dog that 'scoots' along the ground, or twists round on himself, may have blocked glands and veterinary attention should be sought.

Arthritis A very painful degenerative condition in which the joints suffer damage. The dog should be kept active and mobile, and his weight must be controlled. Anti-inflammatory medicines prescribed by a vet can do much to relieve the pain and discomfort.

Asthma This complaint is usually associated with older or obese Staffords. Signs are shortness of breath, wheezy breathing and short, dry coughing. The heart can be affected by this condition. Veterinary attention should be sought.

Aural haematoma A swelling of the ear flap caused by internal bleeding. An affected dog will continuously shake his head and kick at the affected ear with his back leg. Veterinary attention should be sought.

Bad breath This is unpleasant and needs to be dealt with. It may be caused by poor mouth hygiene or a stomach disorder. Poor care of the teeth and gums can cause bad breath. Teeth cleaning solutions are readily available and your vet can advise you.

Bee and wasp stings Bee stings can be very dangerous for a Staffordshire Bull Terrier. They cause great pain and may even result in a state of shock. In severe cases urgent veterinary attention may be required. In the first instance treat with aspirin to help ease the pain and apply TCP or a similar solution (available from pharmacies) to the sting to assist in reducing the swelling.

Staffords tend to snap at wasps in flight during the summer months and can get badly stung on the mouth, tongue and nose. This can cause a lot of pain, and can be dangerous if swelling occurs. At the end of the summer it is not unusual for a Stafford to tread on a drowsy wasp on the ground and get stung on his feet. TCP should be immediately swabbed onto the sting to help reduce the swelling, or the affected foot can be immersed in a bowl containing the same liquid.

Bilious attacks The signs of a bilious attack are vomiting, nausea and general debility. If the dog's temperature is lowered, then veterinary attention should be sought immediately. If the temperature is normal, the dog can be looked after at home. Withhold food, and keep him warm and quiet. As he recovers, change to a very light diet until he returns to normal health.

Bites A severely bitten dog should be taken to the vet without delay. Minor wounds can be treated with iodine or TCP solutions.

Bronchitis This tends to affect older dogs. A persistent irritation or infection causes a cough to develop, which will eventually become constant. Veterinary attention should be sought.

Burns and scalds In the event of a burn or scald, apply a cold compress and seek veterinary attention. Burns can be caused not only by fires and spillages of hot fat and so on, but also by chemical or electrical sources. All require immediate treatment by a vet.

Canker This condition affects the ears. It is painful and very irritating, and an affected dog will constantly shake his head. He may also hold his head to one side. Generally canker occurs when the ear channel becomes blocked with a dark brown waxy substance that may produce an obnoxious discharge. Ear drops can cure the problem, and the ear must be gently cleaned. This type of discharge may also be caused by ear mites. Veterinary attention should be sought.

Cataracts   This problem mainly occurs in older Staffords and can affect one or both eyes. The eye appears opaque and greyish. Cataracts will eventually cause blindness, but surgery can be successful. See also **Hereditary cataracts**.

Choking   Choking can quickly result in death unless immediate action is taken to remove the offending article from the dog's throat. If the article can be seen, try to hook it out with a finger. You may be bitten, but you may just save the dog's life. As Staffords have such powerful jaws, pay close attention to what they are allowed to play with. Avoid giving them cheap, destructible toys, bones and large lumps of gristly meat, and try to keep children's toys out of reach.

Cleft palate   This is a congenital deformity (present at birth). Instead of being flat, the roof of the mouth (palate) is open (cleft). The puppy will be unable to form a vacuum in his mouth, and thus will not be able to suckle properly. Any milk he takes in will bubble out through his nostrils. Although surgery has been known to be successful, the best option is probably to have the puppy put to sleep to prevent further suffering. See also **Hare lip**.

Collapse   A collapsed dog must be laid gently on his right side and kept warm. Veterinary attention must be sought immediately. If the dog is unconscious, do not attempt to administer anything orally, but ensure his tongue is pulled gently forward and cannot fall to the back of his throat.

Conjunctivitis   This is a disease affecting the eyes and is occasionally found in Staffordshire Bull Terriers. There is an irritating discharge and the whites of the eyes appear red and inflamed. Possible causes include viruses, bacteria, chemicals and foreign bodies. It is not necessarily a serious condition but it is always best to seek veterinary advice.

Constipation   This can be very stressful for a dog and must be fully investigated to determine the cause. Incorrect diet is often the reason but there may be an internal obstruction. Veterinary attention should be sought.

Cystitis   An inflammation of the bladder, more commonly found in bitches. Signs include increased frequency of urination, straining and even sometimes blood in the urine. Encourage the dog to drink as much as possible to help flush out the discomfort. Your vet may prescribe antibiotics.

Cysts   Interdigital cysts are very painful, inflamed swellings which develop between the dog's toes and can cause lameness. Such cysts may result from a deep bacterial infection, or from damage to the skin, either through a specific injury such as grass seed penetration or possibly even through walking on salt-covered roads in winter. Daily bathing of the affected paw in warm water containing a mild disinfectant may help to bring the cyst to a head and burst. If the condition persists, veterinary attention should be sought.

Dandruff   Dogs occasionally produce dandruff due to the constant shedding of old skin. Regular daily grooming will eliminate the problem.

Demodectic mange   This is caused by parasitic mites that are passed from a bitch to her newborn puppies and results in patches of hair loss. It can be difficult to treat in severe cases. Some Stafford puppies suffer from patchy hair loss while they are teething. This is sometimes misdiagnosed as demodectic mange, but it almost inevitably clears up completely once the adult teeth have come through.

Accidents, Ailments and Diseases

Dental tartar Left untreated, plaque on the teeth may cause various unpleasant problems, such as gum irritation, gum recession, pain and bad breath, and can ultimately lead to loss of teeth. Regular tooth brushing and hard chews will help, as will a good healthy diet.

Dermatitis Inflammation and irritation of the skin, causing itching and pus-filled lesions. Veterinary attention should be sought. Treatment involves the application of antiseptic creams that must be prescribed by a vet.

Diabetes The most common form of diabetes in dogs is sugar diabetes (diabetes mellitus). The pancreas manufactures insulin, which controls sugar levels. If insufficient insulin is produced, then sugar levels in blood and urine rise. Signs include increased thirst, weight loss, lethargy and the passing of large quantities of urine. Without treatment to regulate his sugar levels, a dog may go into a diabetic coma. Veterinary attention must be sought.

Diarrhoea Often caused by no more than a mild bowel infection, diarrhoea can also result from a change of diet imposed too rapidly. If the problem persists for more than two or three days, veterinary attention should be sought.

Distemper (hard-pad) A contagious and highly infectious serious illness with no known cure, it affects a dog's respiratory and nervous systems. This killer disease has been brought under control with the use of vaccines. A puppy's initial injections protect him from it.

Eclampsia Most at risk are bitches with large litters of puppies, and the condition results from the sudden deficiency of calcium in the blood due to heavy demands from the puppies for large amounts of milk. Signs include loss of balance on rising, a changed expression and increasing unsteadiness. If you suspect eclampsia, call the vet immediately. A large dose of calcium will soon have the bitch back on her feet, and after a rest she will be able to return to feeding her puppies. She may require a further dose a few hours later, and her condition during this period should be closely monitored. The puppies during this time will probably need a supplementary feed of lactol, as advised by the vet.

Electrocution If a dog chews through an electric cable and is electrocuted, DO NOT TOUCH HIM UNTIL THE POWER IS TURNED OFF. If he is not breathing, begin artificial respiration. Keep him warm and contact the vet for advice.

Entropion An inherited condition of the eye in which the edge of the eyelid rolls inwards so that the lashes rub against the surface of the eye. This will cause tears, irritation and soreness. Surgery will solve the problem.

Epilepsy An epileptic fit comes on suddenly and without warning. The affected dog will fall to the ground and thrash around uncontrollably. He may urinate and defecate. There is little that can be done to assist, other than to keep him as comfortable as possible and hold his tongue forward so that it doesn't block his airway. Most dogs recover after a short time and return to normality without appearing to suffer any side-effects. There is no cure for epilepsy in dogs and further attacks are likely to occur in the future. Veterinary attention must be sought.

Fits and Seizures *See* **Epilepsy**.

Flatulence This is almost always diet-related, and can be cured by adjusting the diet to one that is highly digestible and produces less waste. The addition of bran to the food will often help
.
Foreign bodies Thorns, splinters and grass seeds can become lodged in the pad of a dog, causing lameness and pain. It is usually a fairly easy task to examine the pad and gently remove the offending object. Treat the entry point with antiseptic.

Gastro-enteritis Inflammation of the stomach is a most unpleasant and painful complaint, which can become very serious if left untreated. An affected dog will vomit up a great deal of thick mucus-like froth. Blood-flecked diarrhoea can also be expected, and there may be dark blood in the stools. Veterinary attention must be sought. The dog should be given a light milky diet to assist recovery.

Hare Lip This is a congenital fault occasionally seen in new-born puppies. Instead of the two halves of the upper lip being joined together, there is an open split which prevents effective suckling. Surgery is required to correct the deformity. *See also* **Cleft palate**.

Heart diseases Any indications of heart problems, such as excessive panting and coughing, an intolerance of exercise and general weakness, should be investigated.

Heartworm disease This disease is spread by mosquitos and is currently far more prevalent in the United States than in Britain, but the increasing incidence of cases is causing concern. An affected dog will have the worms in the heart and the blood vessels of the lungs. Failure to treat the problem can result in a decline in health, leading to heart failure and death. Watch out for excessive tiredness, a lack of enthusiasm for exercise and deep coughing. A concerned owner should immediately consult a vet.

Heat stroke This should be regarded as an emergency and treated without delay. It occurs in hot weather, with the victim showing deep distress, excessive panting and possible collapse, leading in extreme cases to rapid death. Run cold water gently over his body or place him in a shallow cold bath until his temperature returns to normal. Offer him a drink of water containing salt (a teaspoon of salt to half a litre of water) and treat for shock if necessary.

Prevention is always better than cure! Use common sense and keep your Stafford out of the sun on hot days. Dogs can only perspire through the mouth and the pads of the paws. They cannot tolerate being left in a car on a hot day and if not rescued can quickly collapse and possibly die.

Hepatitis-Canine An infectious and acute liver infection that is potentially fatal. Dogs that recover from hepatitis can still pass on the infection in their urine for many months afterwards. The puppy's initial vaccinations protect against this lethal and debilitating disease.

Hereditary cataracts (HC) This is an inherited gene mutation that causes progressive blindness in both eyes of a puppy soon after birth. The eyes of an affected puppy will appear normal when they open 10 to 12 days after birth. The cataracts will start to appear some weeks or even months later, and progressive deterioration to total blindness will occur during the next few years.

A puppy can only be affected if both parents are carriers of the disease, even if they themselves show no abnormality in their eyes. Thanks to the work of the Animal Health Trust in Newmarket, England, there is now a DNA test for hereditary cataracts. Each puppy tested will be categorized as 'clear', 'carrier' or 'affected'. All results are recorded by the Kennel Club. In a litter born from 'clear' parents all the puppies will be 'hereditary clear' and will not require testing for the disease. A litter from one 'clear' parent and one 'carrier' will probably consist of some 'clear' puppies and some 'carriers'. The whole litter will need to be tested. A decision will need to be made whether to breed from known 'carriers'. Breeding from only 'clear' dogs is the most sensible way forward.

Hip dysplasia A condition affecting many breeds of dogs that results in pain, lameness and eventual arthritis. It is not common in Staffordshire Bull Terriers, but it does occasionally occur. Anyone thinking of buying a puppy is advised to check on the hip status of both parents. X-rays show the extent of any problem, and a resulting score is awarded by a specialist. Responsible breeders will be able to tell you the hip scores of their dogs.

Accidents, Ailments and Diseases

Playtime!

Accidents, Ailments and Diseases

Indigestion A minor problem often caused by over-eating or by eating unsuitable foods. Do not feed the affected dog for a few hours, and then offer light, suitable meals until the problem is resolved.

Kennel cough A highly contagious disease that is spread by droplets and usually affects dogs housed together, as in boarding kennels and at dog shows. An affected dog will produce a dry and hacking cough, often accompanied by an unpleasant discharge from nose and eyes. An incubation period of seven days is usual. Rest and antibiotics are usually prescribed to clear up the disease.

L2HGA (Hydroxyglutaric Aciduria) This is a most uncommon disease in Staffordshire Bull Terriers but it has been linked with certain blood-lines. It is recessively inherited (both parents must be carriers of the recessive gene to produce affected puppies). The symptoms are alarming. An affected dog will display serious behavioural changes. Seizures, dementia, unsteady gait, anxiety attacks, muscular stiffness and tremors can all affect a sufferer. Fortunately, as with hereditary cataracts, a genetic test has been determined that can identify carriers of the faulty gene. No responsible breeder should breed from parents which have not been tested and identified as 'clear', unless they are registered as 'hereditary clear' in Kennel Club documentation.

Leptospirosis A bacterial disease that affects the liver and kidneys. It can be passed on via urine from an infected animal, and living in an environment inhabited by rats, foxes and other forms of wildlife can promote the possibility of infection. The initial puppy vaccinations include the necessary protection from this disease.

Lumps and bumps Most dogs will suffer from lumps and bumps developing on the surface of the skin at some time. Any cysts, abscesses or raised protrusions should be closely watched. If they persist or grow larger, surgery may become necessary to remove them. In the older dog it is probably best to leave them alone unless they are causing obvious illness or discomfort.

Mastitis An infection of the mammary glands that sometimes occurs in lactating bitches. The glands swell up and become hard and painful. Veterinary attention should be sought. In older unspayed bitches usually benign tumours may form. Because of the danger of malignancy, any lump should be considered for surgical removal to avoid the possibility of spreading to other organs.

Mouth tumours Tumours in the mouth can be malignant and rapidly spread to other organs. Signs may include difficulty in eating, bleeding from the mouth and bad breath. Veterinary attention should be sought.

Nose bleeds Bleeding from the nose can be caused by an impact with something, by violent sneezing or by ulceration of the linings within the nose. An ice pack applied to the nose is usually sufficient to stop the bleeding but if the problem persists you should consult a vet.

Obesity A Stafford should never be allowed to become overweight. The Kennel Club Breed Standard calls for an adult dog to weigh 28–38lb (13–17kg) and an adult bitch to weigh 24–34lb (11–15.4kg). The heavier the dog, the further he moves away from the concept of a 'muscular, active and agile' Stafford. Extra weight also places an extra burden upon the general well-being and health of the dog. Feeding the correct diet and taking sufficient exercise is the best action to take.

Parvovirus An acute and highly contagious viral infection that produces life-threatening illness. It is much more common in puppies than in adults. It causes vomiting, abdominal pain and blood-flecked diarrhoea, resulting in thin, weak and dehydrated puppies. It can kill within twenty-four hours of infection, so any affected dogs must be isolated from all other dogs to help prevent the spread of infection. Medication and fluids to replace losses are essential and must be given as soon as possible. Vaccination is essential. Protection for young puppies is included in their initial vaccinations.

Patella dislocation The patella is a small bone situated in front of the stifle and is the equivalent of a knee-cap in humans. A patella that slips in and out of place will cause a dog to hop and limp painfully. It is not a serious problem in Staffordshire Bull Terriers, but it is more likely to occur in a dog with straight stifles than in one with well bent stifles. It may occur in young Stafford puppies, but lessens in severity as they mature and build up muscles in the legs, and may disappear entirely as they become adult. A persistent progressive slipping of the patella that does not improve may require corrective surgery.

Perverted appetite Some dogs tend to eat their own stools or those of other dogs. Often they grow out of the habit but prevention is the best solution. Whenever possible, keep the offending dog away from areas that other dogs have utilized for their toilet, and always clean up after your own dog immediately. It may be provoked by a dietary deficiency.

PHPV (Persistent hyperplastic primary vitreous) This is a progressive congenital disease that is present at birth. It can be detected by ophthalmic screening from the age of six weeks. The condition will not improve, and in severe cases can result in blindness. This is rare in Staffords.

Pneumonia An infection of the lungs most often caused by viruses and bacteria. The signs include laboured or rapid breathing, a raised temperature, coughing and a nasal discharge. Pneumonia is always dangerous and needs to be treated by a vet.

Poisoning Dogs can be poisoned by many substances. It is vital to contact a vet immediately with all the information you can find. Prompt action can save a dog's life. Always follow the instructions given to you. Collect samples of any suspected materials or liquids for identification or analysis by the vet. If possible, retain a sample of any expelled vomit for analysis by the vet.

Pyometra This is a disease that affects the uterus of a bitch. Generally it occurs in older bitches but it can be found in younger bitches, whether or not they have had puppies. The cause is a hormone imbalance. In a bitch affected by pyometra, fluid and mucus will accumulate and build up. If bacteria then invade the uterus, this may lead to acute illness: the onset of pyometra. There are two types. In 'open pyometra' a bloodstained discharge is ejected that can be mistaken for a bitch coming into season unexpectedly. In 'closed pyometra' no discharge is present and the bitch is obviously ill. Pyometra can be fatal. Medical treatment is available but the recommendation is to have a hysterectomy, especially if a bitch is no longer breeding.

Rabies A viral disease sometimes known as hydrophobia. It is an acute infectious disease that can affect any warm-blooded animal, including humans. It is transferred by saliva, and can only be passed on by an infected animal's bite. On entering the bloodstream, the virus attacks the victim's nervous system and brain. Inflammation of the brain follows, bringing on horrendous symptoms which will eventually lead to death. There is no cure but vaccinations are available to prevent the disease.

Fortunately, due to stringent quarantine laws, the United Kingdom has been free of rabies for many years. The pet passport scheme now allows pets and show animals to move between Europe and the UK, with strict controls in place to ensure that all the required regulations – including rabies vaccinations – are fully complied with.

Ringworm A fungal infection of the hairs and skin that causes bald patches. Fortunately it is rare in Staffordshire Bull Terriers. If it is discovered in a dog, contact a vet immediately as it is easily transferable to people and especially children.

Accidents, Ailments and Diseases

Snake bites The adder is only venomous snake to be found in the British Isles. Left untreated, the venom can prove fatal. The bite is particularly painful and a lot of swelling can be produced. A dog, especially if bitten on the head, will require immediate veterinary attention. Owners of Staffords living in country and heathland areas need to be aware that their dogs may be at risk of getting bitten when sniffing out an adder in undergrowth, or if they disturb one found basking on pathways.

Stings *See* **Bee and wasp stings**.

Ticks Ticks can be picked up in parks, gardens and long grass, and during hot weather it is advisable to avoid woodland areas or moorland where sheep or cattle have been grazed. Ticks anchor themselves to the skin of a dog and use their mouthparts to suck blood, eventually swelling up to the size of a pea. If you find one on your dog, do not attempt to pull it off as you may not be able to remove the whole tick. Always seek expert advice regarding removal. Certain spot-on flea treatments will also kill ticks. Your vet will be able to advise you.

10 SHOWING YOUR STAFFORDSHIRE BULL TERRIER

Delighted! My puppy won her class.

Winners on the day.

Showing dogs is a hugely popular pursuit and every weekend dedicated people travel all over the country to compete with their show dogs. The Staffordshire Bull Terrier is one of the most popular of all the pedigree breeds. For newcomers to the breed, watching Staffords at a show will open up a whole new world for them. And for owners, actively showing their Stafford for the first time may well be the first step on the road to a lifelong hobby.

For the owners of Kennel Club registered pedigree Staffords in the United Kingdom a good selection of shows is available to them. There are numerous General Championship shows, and large shows such as Crufts. These cater for most breeds and will almost certainly include classes for Staffordshire Bull Terriers. In addition, the various Staffordshire Bull Terrier breed clubs and societies each hold their own shows for Staffords only. Generally each club holds two or three shows each year, varying from Championship shows to members only shows and open shows. If you can't find one of these, then all over the country many show clubs and societies hold open shows that will include classes for Staffords to compete in. So there is plenty of choice for competitors.

The one thing all these shows have in common is that they are held by permission of the Kennel Club and are governed by the rules of that organization. This means strict adherence to certain procedures in showing and judging. For example, all prize cards awarded in the classes of every pedigree Kennel Club licensed dog show must clearly give the date of the show and be coloured as follows:

First in class – Red
Second in class – Blue
Third in class – Yellow
Fourth in class (reserve) – Green
Fifth in class (very highly commended) – White
Sixth in class (highly commended) – Pink
Rosettes and other prizes may also be awarded, but these are optional.

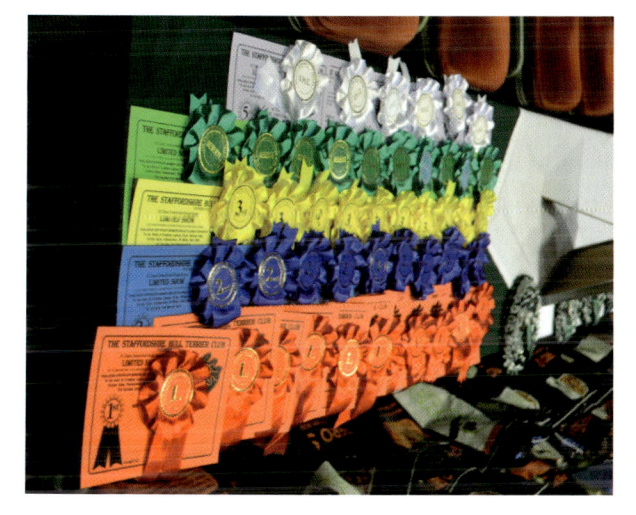

All the rosettes ready for the winners.

GETTING STARTED

You may be entirely new to the breed, and have perhaps bought your first Stafford. And someone with knowledge of the breed has said your dog might do well in the show ring and really ought to be shown. This may inspire you to find out what showing is all about. Why not?

Many first-time exhibitors enter their Stafford in a show just for fun or perhaps to see how their dog compares with others. It is always an enjoyable experience, especially when you find your dog can achieve top awards alongside any of the more experienced and well established competitors. If the judge sees a good dog, he will award it the prize card he feels it merits compared with the other competitors in the class. Don't think that only experts in the breed can reach the top. If your dog really is a good one, he will more than likely be successful in the ring if you learn how to show him to best advantage.

Almost unimaginable pride follows the award of your first prize card! It will almost certainly take pride of place in the home, and your children will proudly show it off to their friends. At this point, it is hardly surprising if the 'show habit' takes hold, and you start looking forward to the next show. And the next. And the greater your success, the more you look forward to the next. As you gain more and more experience, you

A winning young exhibitor, pleased with her dog's result.

Showing your Staffordshire Bull Terrier

may want to try to breed your own puppies for the show ring, and eventually you will become hugely knowledgeable about the breed. This is how most experts started!

SHOW TRAINING FOR YOUR STAFFORD

A newcomer to dog showing will probably already have attended a few dog shows and gained some idea of what is required. Preparation is most important. No one wants to see a complete novice dragging an untrained and bewildered dog around the ring, or for the dog to become so confused that he won't move at all. This is all so embarrassing for the owner that he takes his beloved dog home and never sets foot in a show ring again! If only he had been given some sensible advice, and prepared his dog properly for showing. Given careful preparation and appropriate training, half the battle for success in the show ring is won by the showmanship displayed by a confident dog and the skill of the handler.

There is no great secret to showing. It is simply a matter of preparation and training so that each dog appears to best advantage in the ring. It is a joyous moment for any handler to have his dog responding happily to every command and looking his very best when standing in front of a judge and moving freely around the ring on a loose lead.

A Stafford that has already been properly trained at home will experience no difficulty in adapting to what is required in the show ring. Most of the training can take place at home, but

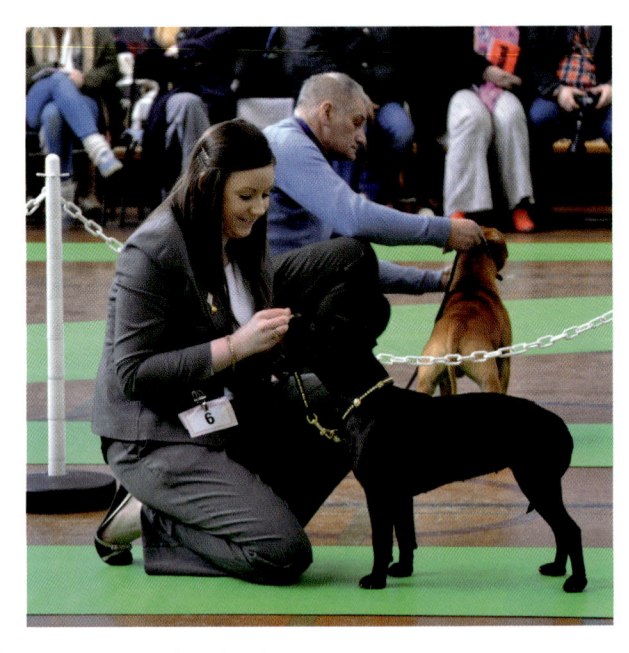

Well trained for the show ring.

Puppies enjoying their time to shine.

much can be gained by attending a ringcraft club. All the Staffordshire Bull Terrier clubs and societies hold ringcraft sessions run by experts who will be able to advise on all aspects of showing a Stafford. There are also general ringcraft clubs that cater for all breeds. At these sessions your Stafford will learn what he must do in the ring, and will be able to socialize with other dogs. This will be of benefit to both dog and owner.

However, it is at home where most of the desired training can take place, with members of the family or friends roped in to help simulate all aspects of what is required from both dog and handler in the ring at a show. Take turns to play the roles of judge and handler. Practise standing the Stafford for examination by the judge, and teach the dog to move freely on the lead, but always under control. It is all great fun! The dog will learn to respond to praise and treats and will look forward to his regular training sessions.

Trained to walk properly with confidence.

In addition to basic training, the show Stafford need to respond instantly to a few simple commands, including 'Stand!', 'Teeth!', 'Steady!', 'Walk!' and 'Turn!' These commands should always be delivered in a firm, calm and confident tone. You do not need to raise your voice: a dog's hearing is far superior to a person's and he can pick out your voice even in the noise and bustle of a show ring. Use whatever words of command you prefer, but only apply them for one particular requirement. Never vary them as this will only confuse your dog. He will not understand a babble of confusing requests!

The following is a good example of the use of simple commands. When you are told to approach the judge and stand your dog for examination, let the dog know what is required of him with a gentle 'Come!' as you approach and 'Stand!' as you stack him for examination. Take your time to ensure he is presented to his best. Using a command such as 'Gently', make sure the dog's feet are all correctly placed so he is standing in a four-square stance and that his topline is as level as possible. Check that his front is displayed to advantage, with his head poised and looking directly ahead towards the judge. Regularly repeat your gentle 'Stand!' command throughout the examination. When the judge examines the dog's head, he will need to check the bite. To assist with this, and prepare the dog, give the gentle command 'Teeth!' When the judge has completed his hands-on examination, he will instruct you to move the dog so he can assess his movement. Give a slight tug on the lead and the command 'Steady!', and then 'Walk!' as you start to move across the ring at a controlled brisk pace. A further 'Steady!' may be required if the dog wanders from a straight line or impulsively tries to forge ahead. Once controlled, it will be 'Walk!', followed when required by 'Turn!' This is followed by another 'Walk!' command as you return to the judge. Give a slight tug on the lead and a 'Steady!' command to stop the walk, and be ready for any final assessment by the judge before returning to your place in the line-up. A routine of regular practice at home and always using the same commands will pay handsome dividends. A Stafford well prepared for the show

Showing your Staffordshire Bull Terrier

ring will show at his best for you, and will not let you down. Knowing this will greatly increase your confidence, enabling the best possible performance from handler and dog.

SHOW REQUIREMENTS

All Kennel Club licensed shows have printed schedules that clearly set out all the relevant rules and regulations. They also include application forms that must be completed in order to enter the show. The closing date for entries will be clearly stated in the schedule. Miss this important date and your entry will not be accepted.

Schedules for shows can be easily obtained. If you belong to the organizing club, then a schedule will normally be sent to you automatically by post. Other shows will be advertised in the weekly dog press and you can apply for a schedule direct from the stated show authority.

Schedules for forthcoming shows are often available at dog shows, dog training clubs and canine events. They may be posted as a matter of course to anyone who has competed at a recent show held by the organizing club. In many cases, schedules for forthcoming shows can be downloaded from the internet.

Included with every schedule will be the entry form. This must be completed in full, with the required information clearly printed in block capitals. The dog's name must be the exact name registered at the Kennel Club. (NB: the 'ATC No.' in the registered name of dog section applies only to dogs entered by exhibitors from outside the United Kingdom.) Once completed, the entry form must be signed and dated by the registered

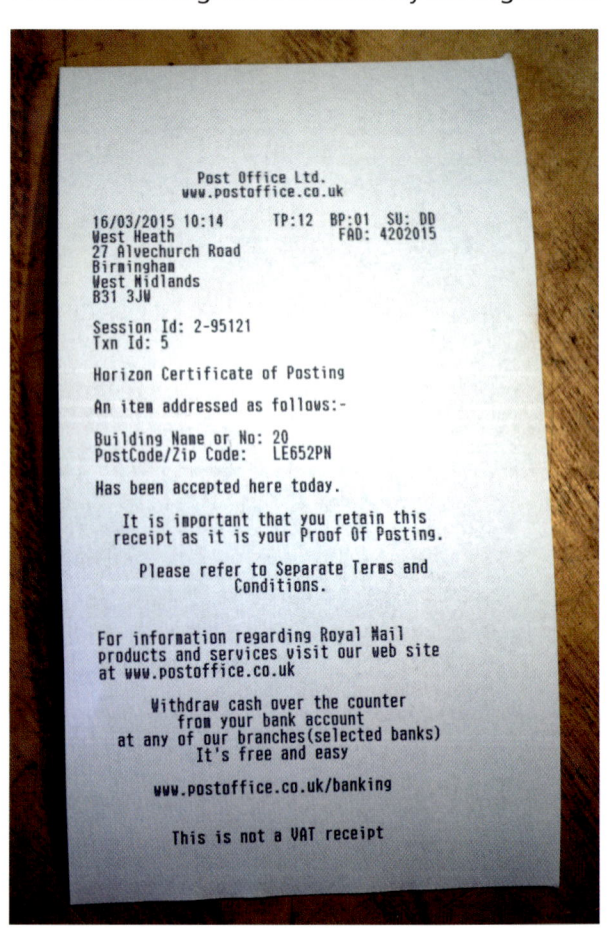

A typical show schedule.

Proof of Postage from the Post Office should be kept for confirmation of your postal entry.

owner of the dog and sent to the named show authority, along with payment for the cost of entries and fees. Do not forget to obtain proof of posting of your entry. You will be very disappointed if you arrive at the show and find your entry has for some reason not been received. A visit to the show secretary with your post office proof of posting certificate should resolve the problem.

On the entry form you must include the class number(s) in which you want to enter your Stafford. The class numbers will be clearly shown in the schedule for the event. It is up to you to make sure your Stafford is eligible for each class you enter, especially in those classes where age limits are imposed, such as Minor Puppy, Puppy, Junior and Yearling. The following are the typical Kennel Club requirements for eligibility:

Minor Puppy: for dogs aged six months but not exceeding nine calendar months of age on the first day of the show.
Puppy: for dogs of six months but not exceeding twelve calendar months of age on the first day of the show.
Junior: for dogs of six months but not exceeding eighteen calendar months of age on the first day of the show.
Yearling: for dogs of twelve months but not exceeding twenty-four calendar months of age on the first day of the show.
Maiden: for dogs which have not won a Challenge Certificate or a first prize at an Open or Championship Show (Minor Puppy, Special Minor Puppy, Puppy and Special Puppy classes excepted, whether restricted or not).
Novice: for dogs which have not won a Challenge Certificate or three or more first prizes at Open or Championship Shows in Graduate, Post Graduate, Minor Limit, Mid Limit and Open classes, whether restricted or not, where Challenge Certificates were offered to the breed.
Graduate: for dogs which have not won a Challenge Certificate or four or more first prizes at Championship Shows in Graduate, Post Graduate, Minor Limit, Mid Limit, Limit and Open classes, whether restricted or not, where Challenge Certificates were offered to the breed.
Post Graduate: for dogs which have not won a Challenge Certificate or five or more first prizes at Championship Shows in Post Graduate, Minor Limit, Mid Limit and Open classes, whether restricted or not, where Challenge Certificates were offered to the breed.
Limit: for dogs which have not become Show Champions under Kennel Club regulations or under the rules of any governing body recognized by the Kennel Club or won seven or more first prizes in all at Championship Shows in Limit or Open classes, confined to the breed, whether restricted or not, at shows where Challenge Certificates were offered for the breed.
Open: for all dogs of the breeds for which the class is provided and which are eligible for entry at the show.
Veteran: for dogs of not less than seven years of age on the first day of the show.
Not for Competition: societies may at their discretion accept Not for Competition entries from breeds of dog not included within the title of the society, and at shows held over more than one day such entries may be accepted on any day from any breed.

It is always best to obtain a schedule for any show you wish to enter. It will contain directions to the venue, times of opening and commencement of judging, contact details and much useful information about the show. Stafford club show schedules will also give some information about

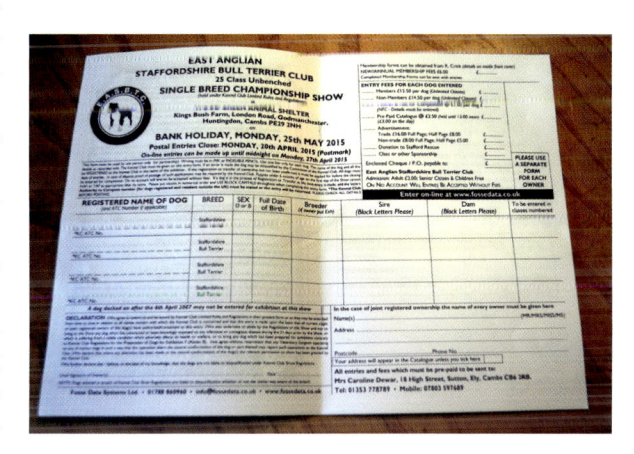

Typical entry form for a show.

Showing your Staffordshire Bull Terrier

the judges and their experience and background in the breed.

For many shows these days you don't need to enter by post but can enter and settle payment for your entries online. You won't receive a schedule through this method but you should be able to download one. The information you provide online will be exactly the same as for entering by post. One big advantage of using this facility is that you will receive an immediate acknowledgement that your entries have been received, are accepted and being processed.

AT THE SHOW

There are two sides to holding a dog show. There is the formal, procedural side, which is concerned with the implementation and strict observance of the rules and regulations of the Kennel Club. This is in the main the function of the officers and committee of the clubs or society staging the show. An exhibitor must take the regulations into account when making his entry, but at the show he will take a far more informal approach and will be much more concerned with actually preparing his dog for showing. As long as the conventions in the ring are observed, an exhibitor is free to choose how to show his dog to best advantage. He will have his make his own choices about this.

Before setting off to a show, always plan well in advance. Don't make silly mistakes like taking the wrong dog to the show or even arriving for a show on the wrong day – we have done this in the past! Make sure you have clear directions to get to the show and allow plenty of time for the journey. It is not uncommon for exhibitors to arrive late and miss their classes. Make sure

A day out at the show.

Showing your Staffordshire Bull Terrier

Examples of Stafford show sets: collars and leads.

you have all you need for your dog to keep him comfortable throughout the day.

It is very helpful to get your Stafford a show collar and lead for use only for show training and for showing in the ring. He will identify with this as a change from his regular collar, and will quickly learn what it is for. There are many different types of show collars and leads available for Staffords. Many are specifically designed for the purpose and do much to positively identify the individuality of the breed.

Make sure your Stafford is presented correctly. This means he must be clean and well groomed. You should only bath your Stafford if absolutely necessary. If you do have to give him a bath, do it a couple of days or so before the show to allow time for the coat to settle down. Grooming for a Stafford means no more than a gentle brushing to remove any dead fur. Any untidy growth of fur on the underside of the tail can be trimmed off if necessary. This will help with overall appearance and emphasize that desirable 'pump handle' shape. This is the only acceptable form of trimming for the breed. Find someone who is experienced in doing this properly to help you. Never trim off the whiskers on the dog's face. There is no valid or advantageous reason for their removal and it will not improve the dog's appearance. Nor will it impress a judge.

Try to dress appropriately for the show ring. Above all, it is important that you are comfortable, especially in large classes. It is not a question

Dress should be smart but comfortable. There's no doubt this dog is comfortable!

Showing your Staffordshire Bull Terrier

of formality, but you do need to be smart. Avoid jeans and inappropriate shoes. Choose attire that will enable you to move your Stafford freely and easily to full advantage, and allow you to remain comfortable.

Make sure you are ready with your dog when it is time for your class to be called into the ring. Take the opportunity to watch how the judge is going about his job and what you will be expected to do. For instance, when he is judging movement, he may ask for the handlers to move their dogs straight up and down a couple of times while he moves across to judge the movement from the side. Never obstruct the judge's view of your dog by walking on the wrong side of him. Alternatively, the judge may instruct the handlers to move their dogs in a triangle. Whatever you are asked for, be ready to do it properly.

When you enter the ring with your dog, you will be asked to line up along the sides with the other exhibitors in your class. Leave plenty of space around yourself, where your dog will not be obscured from the judge's view. Be aware of what the judge is doing: some judges like to take an overall look at the dogs before they begin, and it's not helpful if your dog is facing the wrong way!

Likewise, some judges like to send all the dogs in a class around the ring before they line up again. This allows them to take a good look at the general conformation and movement of all the dogs. Be prepared for this and make sure your Stafford walks well under control when dogs are moving in front of and behind him.

Before he starts examining the exhibits, the judge will usually take a walk along the line of dogs and take a good initial look at all of them from the front. He then may sometimes decide to walk round and view them from the back. Be ready for this and be sure to have your dog properly stacked and presented as the judge passes. He may well be making a mental note of the dogs that particularly attract his attention. Make sure your dog is showing himself at his best.

When it is your dog's turn to be called forward, smartly get him into position and presented to best advantage. Never attempt to engage the judge in conversation and stay silent unless spoken to. If the judge asks you a question, reply briefly and courteously and then remain silent. After he has examined and moved your dog, the judge will signal for you to return to your place. Do so smartly and promptly, and do bear in mind that the judge may well keep his eye on your dog until you get back to your place. Keep him calm – it won't help if he starts leaping up and down and generally lacking control.

Well presented and ready for the judge.

The judge will generally take about two minutes to complete the examination of each dog in a class. This may mean you will be in the ring for a long time if the class is large. Don't just stand there and get bored: use it as an opportunity to practise standing your dog. Some handlers give treats to their dogs to help prevent boredom,

Presenting your dog to advantage.

but be careful with this approach. Your dog may become so obsessed about the treats that he won't behave properly when being examined and moved.

When the judge has finished his individual examinations, he will walk along the line as he makes his decision. At this point your dog must be looking his very best. Resist the temptation to fiddle and fuss about trying to adjust his presentation just as the judge comes to look at him. You could well spoil your chances of being placed by hiding his virtues at the wrong moment.

Try to relax! Any nervousness of the handler will be relayed to the dog. Correct ring training will greatly eliminate this problem and give confidence to both dog and handler. You will quickly adapt to and learn the requirements for showing your Stafford. Whether you win the class or not, remember that you will always be taking home the *best* dog at the show!

Ready for the judge's choice.

Showing your Staffordshire Bull Terrier

When the judge has made his selections, there will be winners and losers in every class. In the spirit of the competition always courteously accept the decision of the judge on the day. If your dog has won, enjoy the success but be magnanimous towards your fellow competitors. If your dog has not been placed, congratulate the winners.

Best Puppy!

Best of Breed on the day!

11 JUDGING THE STAFFORDSHIRE BULL TERRIER

There will be newcomers to the world of the Staffordshire Bull Terrier who will one day aspire to become future show judges for the breed. This chapter is aimed at such people and is intended to act as a guide to pass on some of the experiences and observations gained over many years participating in judging the breed. It will focus on the principles involved in the fair and sound assessment of a class of Staffords so that the best dogs are rewarded. All that follows takes full account of the Kennel Club Breed Standard.

There are two types of judges. 'All-rounders' may judge many breeds, guided by their expert knowledge of balance, substance, soundness, conformation and in particular movement of a particular dog. They will not necessarily have an expert knowledge of type in all the breeds they judge. There are notable exceptions, with some all-rounders possessing a thorough knowledge of type in Staffordshire Bull Terriers. All-rounder judges can play an important part in the future of a breed. Through strict observance of the breed standard, they are unlikely to reward conformation exaggerations that may be emerging to the future detriment of a breed.

By far the majority of judges who are chosen to judge Staffordshire Bull Terrier classes in the United Kingdom are 'breed specialist' judges. The breed itself is a numerically strong one, with large entries for Stafford classes at dog shows. A breed specialist judge will be expected to have an expert knowledge of type in the Stafford. As with the all-rounder judges, he will also be expected to have a thorough knowledge of balance, soundness and conformation. He may, however, place a little less emphasis on movement than would the all-rounder judge, concentrating more on type in the dogs he judges.

A newcomer with judging ambitions must firstly learn all about his chosen breed. If his ambitions extend beyond a single breed, and he has the ability, he may later learn about other breeds should he become sufficiently experienced to strive towards becoming an all-rounder judge. What follows is designed to guide those who wish to become a breed specialist judge.

Judging the hindquarters.

GETTING STARTED

Judging Best of Breed.

A judge must have a thorough knowledge of the breed, based on practical experience, and must know the Breed Standard inside out before even contemplating accepting an invitation to judge. He must understand all possible interpretations of the Breed Standard so that he knows exactly what he is looking for. As with other breeds, the Staffordshire Bull Terrier Breed Standard is very much open for individual subjective interpretation. In fact, the only exact specifications indicate the height and weight limits for dogs and bitches. All other parts are open to independent opinion. This is an advantage as slavishly following such artificially imposed restrictions and limitations would inevitably lead to the elimination from consideration of countless numbers of exhibits that do not conform exactly. Instead, the Breed Standard lays down the broad considerations to be observed, and it is up to each judge, using his own knowledge and experience, to assess each dog according to his own interpretation of the requirements of each part of the Breed Standard. No one wants to see the same dog always winning under every judge. Of course, this does not happen, because each judge has his own interpretation of the Breed Standard. Thus a dog that goes unplaced under one judge may gain a top placing a week later under another judge, whose interpretation of the Standard is different. It is not a matter of one being right and one being wrong. They will simply have different opinions regarding such attributes as type, balance, conformation, quality, substance and movement. Of course, a really top class exhibit may be seen to win consistently under any number of different judges.

There is no such thing as a perfect Staffordshire Bull Terrier, although some have come close. In any event it is difficult to imagine that

Who will the judge choose?

all judges, given their own individual interpretations, would agree! Minor faults are inevitably present in even the very best representatives of the breed, and individual judges will have their own opinions on the significance of such faults. Nevertheless every judge should form his opinion on what makes the ideal Stafford in accordance with the stipulations of the Breed Standard, and should carry this image clearly in his mind whenever judging a class of Staffordshire Bull Terriers. His task is to select those dogs that come closest to that ideal, and reward them in their strict order of merit.

A judge must be entirely focused on the job in hand. He should not worry about anything else. A judge who concentrates entirely on his task, and selects those dogs that he believes are the best on the day, will gain respect for an honest performance. There is no other way to gain that respect. As long as he is seen to judge the class honestly and to the best of his ability, it does not matter what other people think about which dogs should have won. Never, under any circumstances, should a judge allow any form of persuasion to influence him to bend the rules. His reputation as a judge depends on his honest performance in the ring. When exhibitors can follow his reasoning, they will begin to see consistency in his choices, and respect him for it.

FAULTS AND VIRTUES

Every Staffordshire Bull Terrier should always be judged on his overall virtues and not on his faults. Clearly there are serious faults, such as lack of correct type, that render an exhibit totally unrepresentative of the breed. There are also certain severe conformation faults, such as a badly overshot or undershot jaw, which must be critically dealt with in a judge's considerations.

Favouring dogs of average quality but no definite faults over top-class dogs that possess minor faults fails to take into account the whole of the dog. This is known as fault judging and can sometimes lead to exceptional specimens with relatively minor faults being relegated to the role of also-rans in favour of dogs of mediocre quality but no actual faults. The danger here is that the winning dogs do not possess any outstanding virtues. This is not the way forward for the future of the breed. A judge will never be wrong if he looks for the dogs with the most good points and sets aside any temptation to

A judge checking the bite.

select the ones with the least wrong with them. The message from the fault clause of the Breed Standard is clear: a dog should not be 'fault judged' alone. Rather, a balance of his overall virtues should be taken fully into consideration, with acknowledgement of whatever faults he may be deemed to possess.

Judging on the good points without full regard to the whole of the dog is also unsound. For example, a Stafford with one outstanding feature but otherwise lacking in overall qualities should not be placed ahead of one that is less appealing but in fact is closer to the Breed Standard.

Some judges become fixated on certain features, and as a result attribute more significance to them than should be the case. These might include, for example, coat colour, eye colour, tail carriage, ear shape or dentition. Condemning an otherwise first-class Stafford due such a feature fixation is unsound as it does not take into consideration the whole of the dog.

JUDGING TO TYPE

The Breed Standard makes no reference to differences in type in Staffordshire Bull Terriers. 'Type' is the sum of all those points that make a dog look like his own breed and no other. As with most breeds, there is a range of different types of Staffords, often conforming to the preferences of their respective owners and breeders. However, there is only one Breed Standard, and all Staffords are judged by its clauses.

A class of bitches.

Judging for the correct substance.

A judge will almost certainly have a preference of his own regarding type, derived from his overall experience in the breed. In fact, he may well be invited to judge because he is known to have a preference for a particular type. However, every judge should go into the ring with an open mind. Demonstrating a preference for a certain type could result in poor-quality dogs winning over good ones.

IN CONCLUSION

There are no hard and fast rules in judging, and each judge forms his own particular approach to the task. A new judge will be on the right path if he always keeps his interpretation of the Breed Standard in mind and sticks to it as he judges. This will enable him to judge the whole of a dog, and not just his good or bad points, and

Congratulations! Veteran Bitch Winner.

then evaluate each dog against the others in the class.

What follows is an example of a judging technique that has proved successful when applied to the assessment of each and every dog in a class of exhibits. It allows every dog to be demonstrably assessed in exactly the same way. Exhibitors may have travelled many miles and gone to considerable expense to show their dog, and they deserve a level playing field. All dogs, regardless of quality, must be given exactly the same treatment as all the others in a class.

There is much to be gained by making a detailed visual assessment of a Stafford before laying a hand on him. At all stages remember to make your assessment of the dog as a whole, viewed from any angle. As an exhibit is being prepared by the handler for presentation, move well to the side and run your eye from tip of nose to tip of tail in one careful sweep. This will take only a

Judging the Staffordshire Bull Terrier

The award of Challenge Certificate and Best of Breed.

couple of seconds. Observe those characteristics you require for your judgement. Note especially the following:

- length, depth, shape and strength of the muzzle; its angulation and relationship to the skull;
- depth and strength of the underjaw; firmness of lips;
- depth and strength of skull;
- definition and depth of the stop;
- length and strength of the neck; the connection to withers and shoulders;
- angulation and muscle development of shoulders;
- development and depth of chest and brisket;
- length, muscle development, and bone construction of forelegs;
- strength and angulation of the pasterns;

145

Judging the Staffordshire Bull Terrier

An overall look at the competitors.

- shape and conformation of the feet; condition of claws;
- sweep up into the loins;
- length of back; levelness of topline;
- angulation of croup;
- bend of stifle;
- development of thighs;
- angulation and length of hock; and
- set of the tail.

Next move to the rear and observe:

- strength and muscle development of hindquarters;

Moving around to look at the hindquarters.

Judging the Staffordshire Bull Terrier

A close study before the selection is made.

- angulation of the hocks;
- length and development of coupling;
- spring of the ribs; and
- length, taper and strength of neck.

Finally move to the front and observe:

- width and depth of skull and muzzle;
- set and shape of eyes and ears;
- strength of foreface and cheek bumps;
- width and depth of chest and brisket;
- angulation, shape and size of feet; and
- straightness, strength and construction of forelegs.

With experience, you will have observed much of what you need to know about the dog even before laying a hand on him. This visual once-over takes very little time but it forms an important part of the overall assessment. Certainly it

A close examination of the dentition.

147

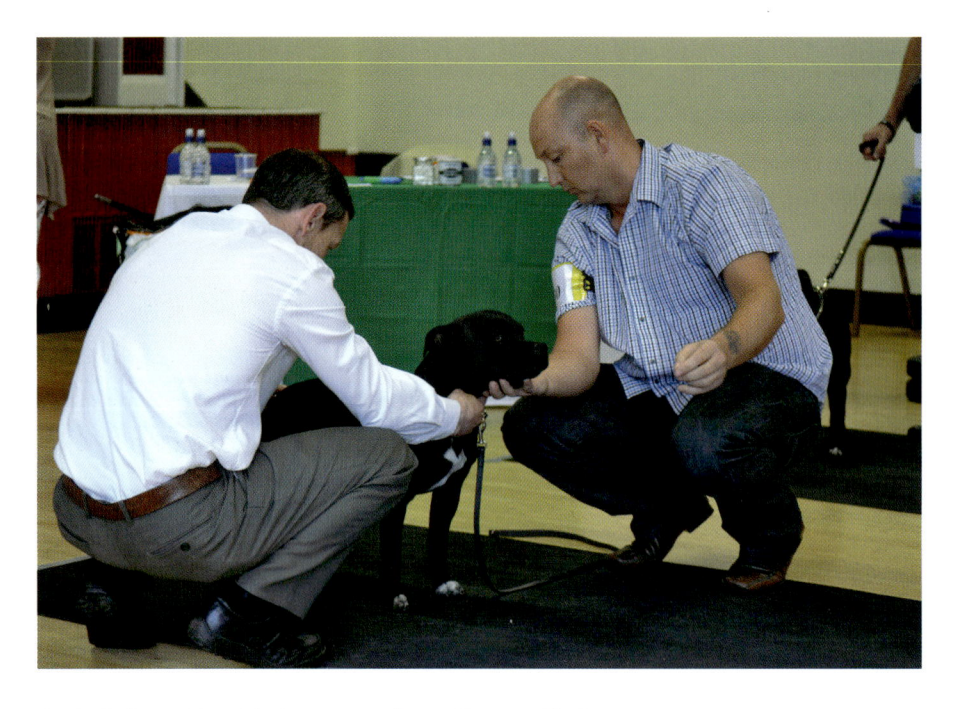

A study from the side to see conformation and balance.

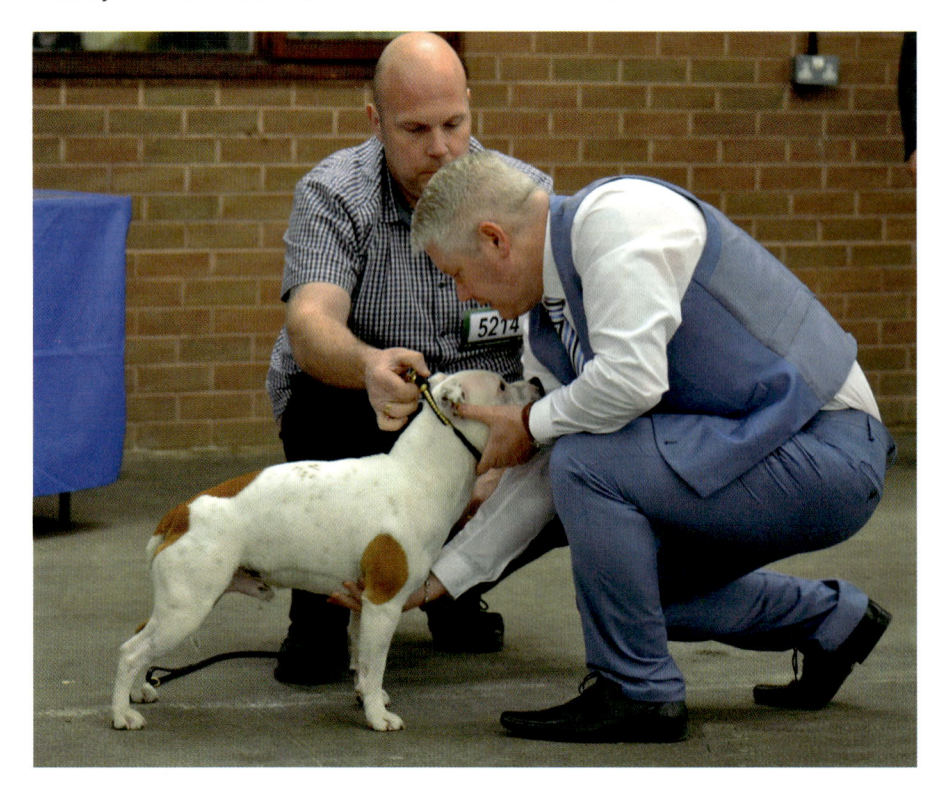

Checking the essential features.

will give a good idea what to look for when you examine the dog physically.

Go forward to the head of the dog. Gently raise the lips and examine the mouth. Check for the size and set of the teeth in the jaws, the presence or otherwise of a scissor bite, and the state of the teeth. Run your hands down the sides of the muzzle to check for strength and development. Check the angulation of the stop and feel for the overall strength of the skull. Check the texture, size and shape of the ears. Place your hands on the dog's shoulders and check his soundness by rocking him gently from side to side.

Go around to the side. Check the position of the shoulder blade by putting one hand on the withers and the other on the point of the shoulder at the lower end of the shoulder blade. You can then check the angle between shoulder and upper arm by running your eye down to the elbow. A well stacked dog can be deceptively posed. Make sure you gently press down at the back of the withers for firmness. Run a hand under

Judging the Staffordshire Bull Terrier

the bottom of chest and brisket to check the sweep up to the loins and then, with a hand on the croup, press down gently but firmly. Do bear in mind that a good handler can conceal faults such as hocks that tend to incline at an angle other than required. All will be revealed when the dog is moved. Check with your hands the muscle of the first and second thighs for development, strength and firmness.

Go around to the back. Check for firmness of the stance and the angulation of the hocks. Run your hands down the neck to check muscle formation and firmness and continue by running the hands along to check the spring of the ribs and the area and length of the coupling. Check the length of the tail by moving it over to the point of the hock, and run a hand down its length to check for any kinks. Do not forget to check the testicles of male dogs.

It seems a lot to do, but really it can all be done in a very short period of time. The last thing to do is check the dog's movement. You can ask for the dog to be moved in a triangle,

Assessing the hindquarters.

Checking for fitness.

149

Judging the Staffordshire Bull Terrier

A quick check of the tail.

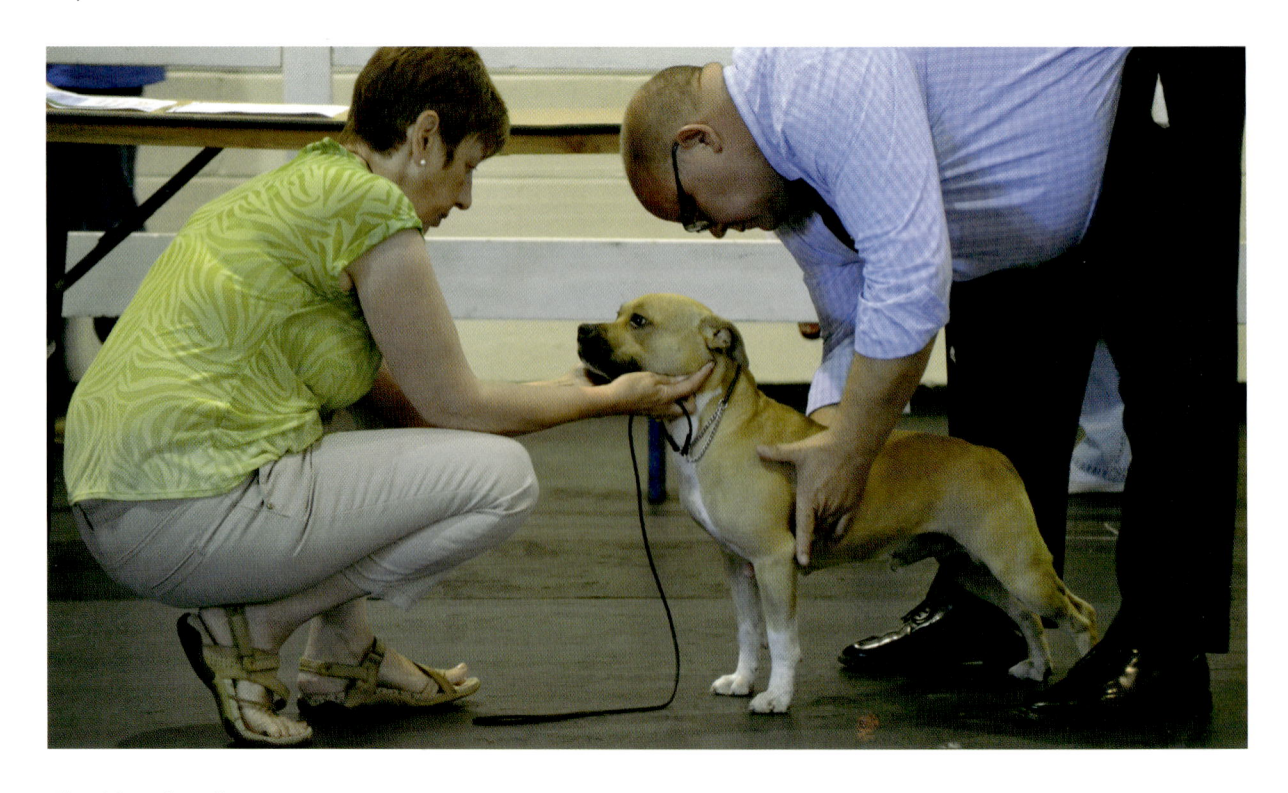

Checking the elbows.

Judging the Staffordshire Bull Terrier

Assessing forward movement.

which has the advantage of displaying the movement without requiring you to move from your judging position. It is important that you assess the movement from the side. Staffords often prove difficult due to their impulsive tendency to drive forward vigorously when asked to move, so they need plenty of space to regain their normal stride. Alternatively you can ask the handler to move straight up and down the ring a couple of times, and position yourself to obtain the best view. Always remember that experienced handlers will stack a dog in order to emphasize his good points and conceal his weak points. It is much more difficult to conceal faults when the dog is on the move.

Position yourself squarely behind the dog to check his gait as he moves up the ring away from you. The back legs should move with a rhythmic spring and with purposeful drive. The hocks should remain parallel, with as little deviation as possible throughout the movement, reaching well forward in a free, powerful and agile gait. There should be no turning in or out of the feet.

As the dog comes back towards you, check for any looseness in the shoulders or for elbows that are out and not close to the sides. The forelegs

Assessing topline, reach and drive from the side.

151

Judging the Staffordshire Bull Terrier

Attracting the dog's attention to observe his expression.

should remain as parallel as possible, moving freely and not turning in or out. Watch out for any weakness in the pasterns.

When you check the movement from the side, it is most important to look for any deviation from a level topline. If there are any faults here, they may not be apparent when the dog is shown standing by a handler. Look for free and powerful unrestricted drive from the hindquarters, and a free unrestricted reach from the forequarters. Any evidence of paddling or a high reaching style is untypical and should be classed as a fault.

Before moving on to the next exhibit, take a quick final overall look at the dog. Perhaps get his attention so you can check his expression.

When all the dogs have been seen in exactly the same way, it will be time to make your choice. Every exhibit will have been judged in the same way and you will gained all the information you need to help make your decisions.

There are no strict rules about how to judge dogs, and every judge is free to establish his own method. The example shown above takes no more than two minutes from start to finish. You may adopt and adapt it, or find your own method. As long as you are confident and comfortable with it, go in the ring and enjoy it.

Good luck!

One of the halls at the Kennel Club Building at Stoneleigh Park: a splendid venue for a show.

12 THE STAFFORDSHIRE BULL TERRIER – IS THIS THE DOG FOR YOU?

'I love my owner' and 'I love my Stafford'.

Go just about anywhere and you will find people with a Staffordshire Bull Terrier. Ask them if they would ever consider another choice of a dog. Almost invariably, they will fondly shake their heads and say no. For them it is a case of once a Stafford owner, always a Stafford owner. They are only too aware of the advantages of their choice.

When you choose a Stafford, what you get, first and foremost, is a great family dog, who will be particularly dedicating to looking after children and the elderly. He will repay your kindness and care with outstanding loyalty and faithfulness. Neither too big nor too small, he will readily adapt to your lifestyle and circumstances.

Happy and content.

The Staffordshire Bull Terrier – Is This the Dog for You?

Happy and content.

Enthusiastic love.

The Staffordshire Bull Terrier – Is This the Dog for You?

Happy and comfortable.

No matter how bad your day has been, a warm and occasionally overwhelming greeting will be waiting for you at home. A short-coated, clean and healthy dog, he is also highly intelligent, and will respond admirably to sensible training with obedience and a devoted willingness to please you. You will be getting a dog that has faith and trust in people, and who will respond enthusiastically to everyone you meet.

What you will not get is a lap-dog. A Stafford is both strong and powerful. Yes, he will jump onto your lap if you let him – probably with an enthusiastic bruising impact. But being a proud dog, he will not be happy about being over-fussed and will not choose to stay there for long.

You will not get a guard dog. A Stafford's love of human beings makes him entirely inappropriate for such purposes. He will more than likely respond enthusiastically to the offer of a titbit from a would-be burglar. He would, however, probably make enough noise to act as sufficient discouragement to a stranger's attempts to break in.

You will not get a dog that will be friendly with other dogs. Other than those in his own home, a Stafford generally does not like other dogs. He has a propensity to fight if he regards the attentions of some dogs as aggressive or challenging. A younger Stafford generally loves to play games with other dogs, but once he has been bitten by a larger dog trying to dominate him, then he will change and he won't take the risk of being bitten again. Always keep your Stafford well under control in public places where other dogs are running freely. If attacked, remember that he is capable of fighting to the finish and that would cause a great deal of trouble.

You will get a strong and impulsive dog. Allowing him to run freely in crowded places is a lazy way of exercising him and is courting disaster. He will act instinctively if he sees another dog or a

The Staffordshire Bull Terrier – Is This the Dog for You?

Staffords need their walks in all weathers.

cat and rush straight after it. This could result in an unwanted fracas or even a serious traffic accident. For safety's sake you must be prepared to keep your Stafford under sensible control in public places.

You will get a dog that needs regular exercise to keep him in the good condition expected of the breed.

So, is the Staffordshire Bull Terrier the dog for you? More than fifty years ago I was heavily influenced by the wording contained in the original 1935 Kennel Club Breed Standard, and I haven't regretted it for a second: 'From the past history of the Staffordshire Bull Terrier, the modern dog draws his character of indomitable courage, high intelligence and tenacity. This coupled with his affection for his friends and children in particular, his off duty quietness and trustworthy stability, makes him the foremost all-purpose dog.'

Whenever I see a Stafford I am reminded of these words and I have never for a moment swerved from my dedication and devotion to this wonderful breed. Perhaps more than anything else, it is these few words that portray exactly what a Staffordshire Bull Terrier really is.

IN CONCLUSION

When presented with the opportunity to write this book, I recognized that here was a chance to do something I really wanted to do, and

The Staffordshire Bull Terrier – Is This the Dog for You?

give something back to the breed I have been involved with for so many years. It was an ideal means of opening a window for newcomer and novice alike to take a look at much that I have experienced with my dogs over the years. My aim was to answer some of the many questions that will doubtless be raised in the quest to gain knowledge of this uniquely outstanding breed.

I have enjoyed writing this book and have put in all I can to give the newcomer to the breed something they will find of true benefit, and I hope I have inspired people in their search for knowledge about our beloved breed: the Staffordshire Bull Terrier.

James Beaufoy
Wyrefare Staffords

Happy exercise.

My choice.

STAFFORDSHIRE BULL TERRIER CLUBS AND SOCIETIES

The following list gives the contact details of the Secretaries of the Staffordshire Bull Terrier Clubs and Societies of Great Britain and Northern Ireland. Information on how to join and become a member, details of the shows to be held, training facilities available and all other events and activities of the Club or Society can be supplied by the Secretary. The list is current at the time of publication. In the event of changes taking place, the details of the current Secretaries can be obtained by contacting the persons listed below or The Kennel Club direct.

Downlands SBTClub
Mr Jamie Mace, 5 Elm Tree Close, Bognor Regis, West Sussex PO21 5BF
01243 821672 or 07927 342414
Jamie@Janastaff.wanadoo.co.uk

East Anglian SBTC
Mrs Leslie McFadyen, The Dog House, Seadyke Lane, Old Leake, Lincs. PE22 9HX
01205 871762
easbtclub@gmail.com

East Midlands SBTClub
Mrs Janet Higgins, 20 Smedley Close, Ashby de la Zouch, Leics. LE65 2PN
01530 563898 07791 434858
Janethiggins1524@sky.com

Merseyside SBTClub
Mr Francis Schofield, 9 Meadowsweet Road, Kirkby, Liverpool. L32 1BT
0151 2086596
Fschofield@live.co.uk

Morecambe Bay & Cumbria SBTClub
Mrs Val Finney, 192 Woodlands Road, St Helens, Merseyside WA11 9DY
01744 753217
sanguliano@talktalk.net

North Eastern SBTClub
Miss Jaci McLauchlan, 8 Darcy Close, Yarm, Stockton-on-Tees TS15 9TA
01642 783948
DarcySBT@aol.com

Northern Ireland SBTClub
Mr John Ryder, 10 Orchard Court, Holywood, County Down, N. Ireland BT18 9QE
028 95910287 or 07712351693
kannechor@gmail.com

Northern Counties SBTClub
Mrs Karen Walrham, 2 Dringshaw, Orchard Park, Hull HU6 9DA
01482 807712
karen@dringshawsbt.karoo.co.uk

North of Scotland SBTClub, Mrs Julie Ann Gray, 18 William Mackie Avenue, Stonehaven, Aberdeenshire AB39 2PQ
01569 760418
julie@staffie.co.uk

North West SBTClub
Ms Claire Crossman, 83 Ainsdale Drive, Ashton-on-Ribble, Preston PR2 1TU
01772 724045 or 07501 215601
pendlestaffclaire@live.co.uk

Staffordshire Bull Terrier Clubs and Societies

Notts & Derby District SBTClub
Mrs Helen Reaney, Highfields, 193 Queen Street,
Chasetown, Burntwood WS7 4TJ
01543 684422 or 07792 558272
Helen.reaney@btinternet.com

Potteries SBTClub
Mrs Sheila Reader, 82 Stanier Street,
Newcastle-under-Lyme, Staffordshire. ST5 2SY
01782 611514
s.reader47@yahoo.co.uk

SBTClub South Wales
Mr Kevin Jones, 31 Westlands, Baglan Moors,
Port Talbot, West Glamorgan, SA12 7DD
01639 821410
maxstakev@hotmail.co.uk

Staffordshire BTClub
Mr Alan Hedges, 54 Lincoln Way, Midway,
Swadlincoate, Derbys DE11 7LB
01283 295483
alan@ramblix.fsnet.co.uk

Scottish SBTClub
Mr Gareth Owen, 43 Garden City, Stoneyburn,
West Lothian EH47 8EJ
01501 763721
Gareth.owen14@gmail.com

Southern Counties SBTSociety
Mrs Nancy Booth, 27 Mornington Road, Canvey
Island, Essex SS8 8BB
01268 511248
ramblestaff@me.com

Western SBTSociety
Mrs Sam Mignano-Fricker, 23 Poplar Road,
Bridgwater, Somerset TA6 4UH
07725 078589
secretary@westernsbts.co.uk

INDEX

abscess 119
acne 119
aaunts 8
anaemia 120
anal disorders 120
arthritis 68, 120
Assured Breeders Scheme 41
aural haematoma (ear swelling) 120
bad breath 120
bee stings 120
benzyl benzoate 59
bilious attacks 120
bites 120
bites – snakes 127
blood tests – ovulation 102
Breed Standard (UK) 15, 18, 20
brisket 30
bull and bear-baiting 8, 9
bull and terriers 9, 12, 14
burns and scalds 120
caesarean operation 113
canine teeth 24
canker 120
car sickness 86
carbohydrates 77
cataracts 121
choke chains 58
choking 121
claws – care 73
cleft palate 121
coat 72
collapse 121
command words 86
commands – show ring 131
conjunctivitis 121
constipation 121
coupling 29
Crib and Rosa 10
Cross Guns Inn 15
croup 29, 30, 32
cystitis 121
cysts 121
dandruff 121
Dangerous Dogs Acts 38
dermatitis 122
diabetes 122
diarrhoea 122
diet – changes 75
distemper – canine 70
distemper (hard pad) 122
Dog Rescue Directory 66
Dunn, Joseph 14, 21
ears – care 72
eclampsia 122
electrocution 122
endorsements 49
entropion 122
epilepsy 122

exercise – daily 74
eyes – care 73
false heat 101
fats 77
fibre 77
fighting pits 11
fits and seizures 122
flatulence 122
fleas 71
food
  BARF 79
  bones 80
  dry 79
  frozen 79
  home prepared 79
  organic 80
  raw meat and biscuit 80
  semi-moist 79
  wet 79
foreign bodies 122
gait 33
gastro-enteritis 123
Gentleman Jim 15
gestation period 106, 109
guard dogs 38
hare lip 123
harness 58
heart diseases 123
heat lamp 108
heat stroke 123
hepatitis – canine 70, 123
hereditary cataract (HC) 123
hip dysplasia 123
hocks 30, 31
in-breeding 97
indigestion 125
judges – 'all rounders' 139
judges – 'breed specialists' 139
Kennel Club registration 49
kennel cough 125
L2HGA (Hyroxyglutaric Aciduria) 125
Lady Eve 15
leptospirosis 70, 125
line-breeding 97
lumps and bumps 125
mammary glands 109, 114
mange – demodectic 121
Mastiff type dogs 7. 8
mastitis 125
Molossus 7
nose – care 73
nose bleeds 125
obesity 125
occiput 23
oestrous or heat 100
Old English Terrier 11
out-crossing – breeding 98

parvoviris – canine 70, 126
pasterns 27
patella dislocation 126
perverted appetite 126
Phoenicians 7
PHPV 126
placenta 112, 113
pneumonia 126
poisoning 126
pricked ears 24
prize cards 129, 130
proteins 77
punishment 88
pyrometra 126
rabies 126
rear pasterns 31
registrations – Kennel Club 39, 96
ringcraft clubs 131
ringworm 126
rose ears 24
scanning 105, 107, 108
scissor bite 24
scratch line 11
season 101
second thighs 30
shoulders – well laid back 27, 28
show classification 132
show schedules 132
silent heat 101
Staffordshire Bull Terrier Club, The 15
Staffordshire Bull Terrier Clubs 39, 40
stifles 30, 31
stings 127
stools – checks 74
stop 21,22
stud dog 98, 99, 100
swabs – ovulation 102
tapeworms 71
tartar – dental 122
teeth – care 72
terms for mating 100
ticks 71, 127
tie – mating 105
topline 29
training aids 93
training classes 82
training commands 90, 91, 92
treats 82, 83, 87
tumours – mouth 125
type 19, 142
under-jaw 24
urination – checks 74
vertebrae formations 29
vitamins and minerals 78
weight – care 74
whelping box 109

160